IS ALLAH (S.W) ONE OR THREE?

By:

Munqidh Bin Mahmoud Assaqqar, PhD

(١)

ACKNOWLEDGMENTS

First, all praise and thanks to Allah - God Almighty. It is with great honor that I present this humble work to my reader, hoping that God Almighty will help him benefit from it, and makes him and me among those who know the truth and among the guided.

Following the tradition of prophet Mohammad (PBUH) in thanking people who did us a favor, I would like to thank the many people who I benefited from in completing this work, and possibly my success in this work was a result of their prayers to God Almighty to help me to do so.

I wish to express my appreciation and gratitude to my noble parents, who have done the greatest favor for me, in continuously fostering and cherishing me. I also extend my appreciation to my faithful wife, for her continuous support, help, and for her standing beside me during the completion of this work.

I would also wholeheartedly like to express my thanks and gratitude to the translation team, who played a major role in enabling this book to reach the English speaking reader, Mr. Mahmoud Salah, the translator, and Mr. Ali Qassem, the proofreader.

Finally, I express my thanks and appreciation to Dr. John Eales, who has done me a great favor by doing the final proofreading. Even though he is of a different faith, he managed to do so, for he is concerned about searching for the truth, and following scientific methods in study and discussion.

I also extend my thanks and appreciation to all my brothers, friends and colleagues, who played any role in the completion of this book.

Munqidh Bin Mahmoud Assaqqar, PhD

<u>INTRODUCTION</u>

(Say: He is Allah, the One and Only; Allah, the Eternal, Absolute; He begetteth not, nor is He begotten; and there is none like unto Him) (Holy Quran, 112: 1- 4)

(Christ the son of Mary was no more than an apostle; many were the apostles that passed away before him. His mother was a woman of truth. They had both to eat their (daily) food. See how Allah doth make His signs clear to them; yet see in what ways they are deluded away from the truth!) (Holy Quran, 5: 75)

(He was no more than a servant: We granted Our favour to him, and We made him an example to the Children of Israel.) (Holy Quran, 43: 59)

(They say, "((Allah)) Most Gracious has begotten a son!" Indeed ye have put forth a thing most monstrous! At it the skies are ready to burst, the earth to split asunder, and the mountains to fall down in utter ruin, That they should invoke a son for ((Allah)) Most Gracious. For it is not consonant with the majesty of ((Allah)) Most Gracious that He should beget a son. Not one of the beings in the heavens and the earth but must come to ((Allah)) Most Gracious as a servant. He does take an account of them (all), and hath numbered them (all) exactly. And everyone of them will come to Him singly on the Day of Judgment.) (Holy Quran, 19: 88 -95)

These noble verses have summarized the Muslim's concept, faith and belief in Allah[1] (S.W)[2], the One and only, and His prophet Jesus

---

[1]- Muslims prefer using the name "Allah", which is one of many beautiful names and it is God Almighty's greatest name, instead of the English word "God". The word "Allah" is pure and unique unlike the English word "God", which can be used in many forms. If we add 's' to the word "God" it becomes "Gods", that is a plural of God. Allah is one and singular, there is no plural of Allah. If we add 'dess' to the word 'God', it becomes 'Goddess', that is a female God. There is nothing like male Allah or female Allah. (taken from: "The Concept of God in Major Religions", Dr. Zakir Abdul Kareem, pp 18) (Added by the proofreader)

[2] - Muslims do not mention the name of Allah without glorification. The letters "S.W" are abbreviations of the two Arabic words "Sobhanahu Wataala", which means, ***"Glory to Him! He is high above all"*** (Holy Quran 17:43). The English meaning of these two words is from the "Meaning of the Holy Quran by Abdullah Yusof Ali". Therefore, in

(PBUH)[1]. He is a noble prophet and a great messenger whom Allah (S.W) sent to declare monotheism, and supported him with signs and guidance.

Monotheism, which is what Mohammad (PBUH) carried to humanity, is the faith and belief of all the prophets (PBUT) before him. **(Not an apostle did we send before thee without this inspiration sent by us to him: that there is no god but I; therefore worship and serve Me.)** (Holy Quran, 21: 25)

However, Christians believe contrary to the Muslims, as they believe that Jesus (PBUH) is the Son of Allah (S.W), and some of them believe that he is Allah (S.W) himself. They also believe that He, (Allah (S.W)) came down from heaven, incarnated, was slapped, suffered and crucified, for the atonement of the sin of humanity, which they inherited from their father Adam.

I question, where did they derive this belief, and is there some evidence in their books that support it? **(Say, "Bring your convincing proof.)** (Holy Quran, 21: 24)

In this third part of my series, considering the importance and the seriousness of this issue, I put forward my important questions, was Jesus (PBUH) a messenger or God? Is Allah (S.W) One or three?

In order to answer these questions, I will search and investigate the Holy Bible, the Old and the New Testaments, supported by the clergymen's and the western free thinker's statements.

O Allah, show and guide us to the truth that we argue about, indeed, you guide, whom you will, to the straight path.

Munqidh Bin Mahmoud Assaqqar, PhD

Makkah, Saudi Arabia / Rabee Awal, 1424 (Lunar year)

Email: munqidh@maktoob.com

---

this book I will use the words "Allah (S.W)" when referring to God Almighty, except for excerpts and quotations.
(Added by the proofreader)
[1]- Muslims also do not mention the name of a Prophet without honoring him with prayer and invocation. The letters "PBUH" are abbreviations of the sentence, "Peace Be Upon Him" when mentioning a prophet, or "Peace Be Upon Her" when mentioning the Pure Virgin Mary, and the letters "PBUT" are contractions of the sentence, "Peace Be Upon Them", when mentioning more than one prophet. (Added by the proofreader)

JESUS CHRIST IN MUSLIM BELIEF

The Muslims' belief in Jesus (PBUH), in summary, is that he is the son of the truthful and honored Mary; he was born miraculously without any male intervention or contact. Allah (S.W) sent him as a prophet and messenger to the Children of Israel, to declare monotheism and to prophesize the coming of the final prophet. Allah (S.W) also supported him with great miracles. Challenging the Jews, who wanted to kill him as was their habit of killing prophets, he continued his mission, and Allah (S.W) saved him from their wicked conspiracy and lifted him to the heavens.

Muslims also believe that Jesus (PBUH) will come back again before the Day of Judgment, calling all to worship Allah (S.W), the One and only, following His statute and Law, breaking the cross and raising the flag of monotheism.

To clarify this belief and for more illustration, we will review the verses of the Holy Quran, that Allah (S.W) has revealed regarding Jesus (PBUH).

The Holy Quran mentions that Allah (S.W) has honored Jesus (PBUH) by making him the son of the pure Virgin Mary, whom Allah (S.W) had chosen above the women of all nations. **Behold! The angels said, "O Mary! Allah hath chosen thee and purified thee- chosen thee above the women of all nations."** (Holy Quran, 3: 42)

It also mentions that, Allah (S.W) honored her with many graces, **"Right graciously did her Lord accept her: He made her grow in purity and beauty: To the care of Zakariya was she assigned. Every time that he entered (her) chamber to see her, he found her supplied with sustenance. He said: "O Mary! Whence (comes) this to you?" She said: "From Allah. for Allah Provides sustenance to whom He pleases without measure."** (Holy Quran, 3: 37), that Zachariah adopted her after her mother took a covenant on herself to give her child to Allah (S.W), and that He ordered her to worship Him. **"O Mary! Worship Thy Lord devoutly: Prostrate thyself, and bow down (in prayer) with those who bow down."** (Holy Quran, 3: 43)

Mary (PBUH) became pregnant with her child after Allah (S.W) had given her a glad tiding by the angel, and He gave him a name. **"Behold! the angels said: "O Mary! Allah giveth thee glad**

tidings of a Word from Him: his name will be Christ Jesus, the son of Mary, held in honor in this world and the Hereafter and of (the company of) those nearest to Allah. (Holy Quran, 3: 45)

The verses declare that Allah (S.W) created this coming child, Jesus (PBUH), by a word from Him, without any human intervention. He created him with no father, and that would not make him divine, as Allah (S.W) also created Adam in an unusual way. **"The similitude of Jesus before Allah is as that of Adam; He created him from dust, and then said to him: "Be". And he was.** (Holy Quran, 3: 59) Allah (S.W) created Both, Jesus and Adam (PBUT) by the word "Be".

The Holy Quran also mentions the birth of this holy child and it was without a father, being his first miracle (PBUH). **"And We made the son of Mary and his mother as a Sign"** (Holy Quran, 23: 50) then Allah (S.W) Made him speak while he was still in his cradle, to refute the Jews' wicked accusation to his mother, the pure virgin. **"They said: "How can we talk to one who is a child in the cradle?" He said, I am indeed a servant of Allah. He hath given me revelation and made me a prophet, and He hath made me blessed wherever I be, and hath enjoined on me prayer and charity as long as I live. (He) hath made me kind to my mother, and not overbearing or miserable, so peace is on me the day I was born, the day that I die, and the day that I shall be raised up to life (again)"**

(Holy Quran, 19: 28 -33)

"He shall speak to the people in childhood and in maturity. And he shall be (of the company) of the righteous." (Holy Quran, 3: 46)

When he (PBUH) grew up as a man, Allah (S.W) sent him as he sent many prophets before him. **"And in their footsteps we sent Jesus the son of Mary".** (Holy Quran, 5: 46)

His message was to complete the message of Moses (PBUH). **"'(I have come to you), to attest the Law which was before me. And to make lawful to you part of what was (before) forbidden to you"** (Holy Quran, 3: 50), therefore, Allah (S.W) had given him the knowledge of the Torah, **"Behold! I taught thee the Book and Wisdom, the Law and the Gospel"** (Holy Quran, 5:

110) and He revealed the Gospel to him (PBUH). **"We sent him the Gospel: therein was guidance and light"** (Holy Quran, 5: 46)

Allah (S.W) had supported Jesus (PBUH) with miracles, and had given him many signs, that were enough to convince his people to believe in him. **"Behold! thou makes out of clay, as it were, the figure of a bird, by My leave, and thou breathes into it and it becomes a bird by My leave, and thou heals those born blind, and the lepers, by My leave. And behold! thou brings forth the dead by My leave."** (Holy Quran, 5: 110)

Moreover, as a support, Allah (S.W) gave him the knowledge of the unseen, **"I declare to you what ye eat, and what ye store in your houses. Surely therein is a Sign for you if ye did believe"** (Holy Quran, 3: 49) and supported him with the Holy Spirit, Gabriel (PBUH). **"We gave Jesus the son of Mary Clear (Signs) and strengthened him with the Holy Spirit."** (Holy Quran, 2: 87)

The Holy Quran illustrates that Jesus' (PBUH) message was for the Children of Israel only, **"And (appoint him) an apostle to the Children of Israel, (with this message): "** (Holy Quran, 3: 49) and he delivered that message to them. **"And remember, Jesus, the son of Mary, said: "O Children of Israel! I am the apostle of Allah (sent) to you, confirming the Law (which came) before me, and giving Glad Tidings of a Messenger to come after me, whose name shall be Ahmad."** (Holy Quran, 61: 6)

The Holy Quran declares Allah's (S.W) warning of committing excesses or exaggerating Jesus (PBUH). **"O People of the Book! Commit no excesses in your religion: Nor say of Allah aught but the truth. Christ Jesus the son of Mary was (no more than) an apostle of Allah, and His Word, which He bestowed on Mary, and a spirit proceeding from Him"** (Holy Quran, 4: 171) and this is his true nature and identity **"Such (was) Jesus the son of Mary: (it is) a statement of truth, about which they (vainly) dispute. It is not befitting to (the majesty of) Allah that He should beget a son. Glory be to Him! when He determines a matter, He only says to it, "Be", and it is."** (Holy Quran, 19: 34-35), for Allah (S.W) Created him by His word (Be), God does not need to have a son, Jesus or any other.

Furthermore, the Holy Quran declares that Jesus (PBUH) did not claim divinity. On the contrary, he will reject and deny everyone who claims his divinity, and that will be when Allah (S.W) asks him: **"And behold! Allah will say: "O Jesus the son of Mary! Didst thou say unto men, worship me and my mother as gods in derogation of Allah.?" He will say: "Glory to Thee! never could I say what I had no right (to say). Had I said such a thing, thou wouldst indeed have known it. Thou knowest what is in my heart, though I know not what is in Thine. For Thou knowest in full all that is hidden. Never said I to them aught except what Thou didst command me to say, 'worship Allah, my Lord and your Lord'; and I was a witness over them whilst I dwelt amongst them; when Thou didst take me up Thou wast the Watcher over them, and Thou art a witness to all things"**. (Holy Quran, 5: 116-117) He (PBUH) would say that, for he is just a man.

Therefore, Christian belief in him as divine, and as a son of God is false. **"Such (was) Jesus the son of Mary: (it is) a statement of truth, about which they (vainly) dispute."** (Holy Quran, 19: 34), **"and the Christians call Christ the son of Allah. That is a saying from their mouth"** (Holy Quran, 9: 30), the verses also condemn those who say that Jesus (PBUH) is Allah (S.W) himself. **"In blasphemy indeed are those that say that Allah is Christ the son of Mary. Say: "Who then hath the least power against Allah, if His will were to destroy Christ the son of Mary, his mother, and all, everyone that is on the earth"?** (Holy Quran, 5:17)

Thus, the belief in this great prophet is one of the pillars of the Muslim faith, and Allah (S.W) will not accept one without this belief. **"The Messenger believeth in what hath been revealed to him from his Lord, as do the men of faith. Each one (of them) believeth in Allah, His angels, His books, and His apostles. "We make no distinction (they say) between one and another of His apostles"** (Holy Quran, 2: 285). May Allah's (S.W) mercy and peace be upon them all!

<u>CHRISTIAN EVIDENCE FOR CHRIST'S DIVINITY</u>

In spite of their various opinions about Jesus (PBUH), Christian sects believe that he is God incarnate,[1] supporting this claim with many passages from both the Old and the New Testaments, which speak of his Divinity. These passages, calling him Lord, God or the Son of God, convey that Allah (S.W) had incarnated in him, and that he had created some creations. They consider that his foretelling about the unknown and his raising of the dead is the greatest evidence of his Divinity.

An Introduction to the Discussion on Christian Evidence for Christ's Divinity

It is important, before we start to discuss this evidence, to mention and consider these following few notes:

1) There is no passage in the entire Bible, Old or New Testaments, where Jesus (PBUH) himself declared divinity or that he asked people to worship him. Furthermore, not one of his contemporaries worshipped him. The Jews considered him as someone who claimed prophethood, some believed him, but the majority of them rejected the entire idea.

There is no base in the Holy Bible for Jesus' (PBUH) divinity. Regarding this, Deedat challenged the Swedish archbishop, in their televised debate saying: "I will put my head in a guillotine if you show me one verse where Jesus himself says 'I am God' or where he says 'Worship me'."

In his book (The Secrets Key), Priest Fender explained why Jesus (PBUH) did not openly declare divinity in the New Testament. He said:

"No one could understand this relationship and unity before his resurrection and ascension. If he did so, they would understand that he is God in a human body... the Jewish high priests wanted to catch him and stone him, the fact is that he did not declare his divinity except by puzzles and parables."[2]

---

[1] - Excluding Jehovah witnesses and some of the Monotheistic Churches, for, they reject the Divinity of Christ and Trinity. Even though they believe in the Holy Bible they did not find any evidence support this dogma, therefore, they rejected it.

[2] - The Truth Revealed, Rahmatullah AlHindy, Vol. 3 pp 718-724.

The fear from the Jews is an unacceptable reason for Allah (S.W) or even for Jesus (PBUH) to hide his identity. He used to face and condemn the Jews every now and then as is recorded in the Gospels. **"But woe to you, scribes and Pharisees, hypocrites, for ye shut up the kingdom of heaven in people's faces, for ye neither enter yourselves, nor allow those who would enter to go in.... *ye* blind guides.... you fools and blind.... Woe to you scribes and Pharisees, hypocrites, for you are like whitewashed tombs, you serpents, you generation of vipers, how can you escape being sentenced to hell?** (Matthew 23/13-34) Surprisingly, how and why did he hide his identity from humanity? Doing so creates misguidance and confusion.

2) Not one of Jesus' (PBUH) disciples considered him God, for none of them worshipped him. In addition, the disciples and Jesus' (PBUH) contemporaries did not think of him as more than a prophet. (I will explain later)

3) The strongest evidence, which Christians present to prove Jesus' (PBUH) divinity, is only in the Gospel according to John and in Paul's Epistles, while the Synoptic do not contain a clear passage proving that.

The fact is that the non-existence of this evidence in the Synoptic was the reason that forced John - or the writer - to write a Gospel about Jesus' (PBUH) Divinity. In this Gospel, we find that he wrote what the others did not write, and that this Gospel is full of metaphors and philosophy, which differs from Jesus' (PBUH) simple environment and style, which made many commoners follow him.

4) The non-existence of a clear passage, which proves Jesus' (PBUH) Divinity in the Synoptic, was the reason that led Christians to fabricate and alter the Bible's editions. An example for that is that they have added the only clear passage that declares the Trinity in the First Epistle of John (John 1, 5:7).

Another example is in Paul's First Epistle to Timothy. The editor's fabrication is so clear. It says, **"great is the mystery of godliness: God was manifest in the flesh".** (Ti 1, 3:16)

This verse, and according to Chrispach, is a fabrication. He said,

"It is a fabrication, as the word 'God' does not exist in the original codex, instead it contains the third person subject pronoun 'He' or the demonstrative pronoun 'That or which' ".

Explaining the reason, history and time for this fabrication, Priest James Anas says,

"What makes the reading with the word 'which' more accurate, is that the old theologians did not mention it among the many verses, which they produced while they were refuting Arius. The reason for that change in the New Greek Manuscripts is the similarity between the two words. They both look alike in writing; the only difference between them is a small hyphen or a little dot. Most probably, the writers added this little line to clarify the meaning, thus, changing the word from 'which' to 'God'. Then it spread over many copies in the middle centuries; conflicting what was found in the ancient copies, which contain only the word 'That'".[1]

If we read Paul's above-mentioned verse correctly, apart from the editor's intended fabrication, we will find that it talks about the appearance of godliness in a living body, but the new translations changed it to evidence for God's incarnation in Jesus (PBUH).

The Catholic Jesuits edition, the Douay-Rhiems Bible, and the Murdock Bible deleted the fabrication and corrected the verse. It reads, **"Great is the mystery of godliness: which was manifest in the flesh".** (Ti 1, 3:16), replacing the word 'God' with the accurate word, 'which'. Consequently, changing the meaning and the evidence for God's incarnation in Jesus (PBUH) had disappeared.

Another example of these fabrications is the translators' alteration in the Epistle of Jude. In the most famous and popular Protestant Edition, the Revised King James Version, we find what would deceive and delude the reader. It reads, **"Now to him that is able to keep you from falling, and to present you faultless before the presence of his glory with exceeding joy, to the only wise God our Savoir, be glory and majesty, dominion and power, both now and ever."** (Jud 1:24-25)

The fact is, that the verse mentions the 'Savior God' that would save people by Jesus' (PBUH) mission and message, but not about Jesus

---

[1] - Methodical Theology, James Anas, pp 206. The Truth Revealed, Vol.2, pp 460.

himself. In the Catholic Jesuits' edition, and in the American Standard Version, we find the verse as follows: **"to the only wise God our Savoir, through Jesus Christ our lord, be glory and majesty, dominion and power"** (Jud 1: 25)

In the Protestant edition, they omit Jesus' name to indicate that he is the Savior and not that he was the way to be saved. It calls Jesus (PBUH) 'the only wise God', but in the Catholic edition, the passage talks about Allah (S.W) 'the only wise God our Savior'. Christians fabricated the verses when they could not find any evidence proving Jesus' divinity (PBUH).

Dear brother, whoever searches for the truth, I invite you to join me in order to study scientifically, together and hand in hand, the Christians' written evidence in which they claim that they prove Jesus' Divinity (PBUH).

There are six categories of this evidence,

1. Verses that attribute divinity and lordship to Jesus (PBUH), which they call "God's titles"

2. Verses mentioning his son-ship to God

3. Verses mentioning God's manifestation in him

4. Verses that attribute God's characteristics to him

5. Verses that attribute God's deeds to him

6. Jesus' miracles as a proof of his Divinity

1- VERSES THAT ATTRIBUTE DIVINITY AND LORDSHIP TO JESUS (PBUH)

Christians present some passages attributing divinity and lordship to Jesus (PBUH), and they believe that these words are evidence for his Divinity. The first is his name "Yashua", which derives from the Hebrew word "yehwa khalas" which means, "God has saved".

Another passage is what comes in the Book of Isaiah, **"For to us a child is born, to us a son is given: and the government shall be upon his shoulder: and his name shall be called Wonderful, Counselor, The mighty God, The everlasting Father, the Prince of Peace."** (Isaiah 9:6).

They also believe that David's description of the coming savior is undisputable proof because David called him "Lord". **"The LORD says to my Lord; Sit at my right hand, until I you're your enemies your footstool. The LORD sends forth from Zion your mighty scepter. Rule in the midst of your enemies! Your people will offer themselves freely on the day of your power, in holy garments; from the womb of the morning, the dew of your youth will be yours. The LORD has sworn and will not change his mind, "You are a priest forever after the order of Melchizedek." "** (Psalms 110: 1-4)

Ibrahim Saeed, an Egyptian priest, says:

"Any one, who is not convinced with Jesus' Divinity after reading Psalm 110, is one of two people. Either he is an illiterate and ignorant, whose eyes are covered with stupidity so he will not be able to see, or he is an arrogant, whose heart is filled with stubbornness and he does not want to see".[1]

There is another passage, which they also believe is proof of Jesus' Divinity, that passage is in the Book of Isaiah, **"Therefore the Lord himself shall give you a sign; Behold, the virgin shall conceive, and bear a son, and shall call his name Immanuel."** (Isaiah 7:14) for the word "Emanuel" means, "God with us".

They believe that Jesus' birth (PBUH) was a fulfillment of this prophecy, as the angel foretold Mary's fiancé, Joseph the Carpenter.

---

[1] - Luke's Gospel Commentary, Ibrahim Saeed, pp 504

"She will bear a son, and you shall call his name Jesus: for he shall save his people from their sins. All this took place to fulfill what the Lord had spoken by the prophet: "Behold, the virgin shall conceive and bear a son, and they shall call his name Immanuel" (which means, God with us). (Matt. 1:18-23) According to Christians, calling him Emanuel, "God with us" is evidence of his divinity.

In addition, they present Paul's, Thomas', and Peter's sayings in the New Testament regarding this issue. **"According to the flesh, is the Christ, who is God over all, blessed forever.** (Rom. 9:5)

"Thomas answered and said to him: 'My Lord and my God'." (John. 20: 28)
"Then Peter took him, and began to rebuke him, saying, "Be it far from you, Lord: this shall never happen to you". (Matt. 16:22)
"As for the word that he sent to Israel, preaching good news of peace through Jesus Christ (he is Lord of all)."(Acts 10:36)

In Revelation, there is another passage in this regard, **"For he is Lord of lords, and King of kings."** (Revelation 17:14)

Names Do Not Prove Their Holders' Divinity

None of these words makes Jesus (PBUH) God. Many of these words are used as names only, and if someone's name is god, that does not make him God. According to the New Testament, people named Paul and Barnabas gods when they had performed some miracles. **"And when the crowds saw what Paul had done, they lifted up their voices, saying in Lycaonian, "The gods have come down to us in the likeness of men!""**(Acts 14:11)

The Romans had the tradition of naming people, who had done something good for the nation, gods. This naming does not change the fact, does not change the creature to a creator, and does not change the mortal servants to immortal gods.

The meaning of Ishmael's name is "God hears", the meaning of Jehoecham is "God raise" and of Joshua is "God saved". These people are not gods, even though they had these names.

We read in the Book of Revelation, **"The one who conquers, I will make him a pillar in the temple of my God. Never shall he go out of it, and I will write on him the name of my God, and the name of the city of my God, the new Jerusalem, which comes down from my God out of heaven, and my own new name."** (Revelation 3:12) and in the Book of Numbers, **"And they shall put my name upon the children of Israel"** (Num. 6:27) but they are not gods.

Was "God", Jesus' (PBUH) name?

Muslims do not accept many of these passages, which the New Testament claims came from Jesus' (PBUH) disciples, as true. They also believe that Christians intentionally fabricated these passages, as we found in the First Epistle of John (5:7). The fabrication and alteration may also happen because of bad and inaccurate translation.

The word "Lord" (capitalized), which we find in the Holy Bible's translations, used to implicate the word "God", but we find that some English translations are using the word "lord (with small "L", which means, "Master" or "Mister". In the French translation, they use the word "Le mait" which means, "teacher", and the same in other translations such as the German, the Italian and the Spanish.

The word "Rab", which came in the Arabic translation, is not new; it is the Aramaic word "Rabbi", which is of Jesus' (PBUH) and his contemporary's Aramaic language. This word, "Rabbi" is used as a respectful attribution to a master or a teacher.

The Gospel according to John mentions that the disciples used to call Jesus "Rabbi" or "Rabbony" and they meant teacher. Mary Magdalene turned to Jesus (PBUH) and said, **"Rabboni; which is to say, Master.... Mary Magdalene came and told the disciples that she had seen the Lord"** (John 20:16-17) in another passage, two of his disciples called him, **"Rabbi, (which means teacher."** (John 1:38)

None of the disciples ever meant "God" when using that word to call Jesus (PBUH). What they really meant was teacher or master. Thus, they considered him like John the Baptist, as they said, **"Lord, teach us to pray, as John taught his disciples."** (Luke 11:1)

Using this word "lord" to mean master, is also common in the Greek language. Stephen Nail said, "The original Greek word that means 'Master', can be used as a way of respect. The prison guard spoke to Paul and Silas calling them rabbi or master. **"And bringing them out, he said: Masters, what must I do, that I may be saved? And they said, Believe in the Lord Jesus Christ, and you shall be saved, and your house."**(Acts, 16:30), and this word is a word of honor".

What proves this explanation is, Paul's words, when he described Jesus (PBUH) as "Rabbi" (lord), but he still put him as a servant of Allah (S.W). **"That the God of our Lord Jesus Christ; the Father of glory, may give you a spirit of wisdom, and revelation in the knowledge of him."** (Eph. 1:17)

Thomas' response was not a direct speech to Jesus (PBUH). When he saw Jesus (PBUH) alive, and he thought he was dead, it was a great surprise for him, so he gave an exclamation, and it was "**My Lord and my God.**" (John. 20: 28)

This meaning may be obscure in some translations, but it is clear in the Greek originals. In the Greek manuscripts, we find the words as follows, "apok-ree'-nom-ahee" which means (that was his reaction).

The proof for this explanation is that Jesus (PBUH) said, in the same paragraph, that he would be ascending to his God. (John 20:17) If Jesus (PBUH) understood Thomas' words as if he meant his divinity, he would not accept it. He refused even calling him good, for once, when his disciple called him so, he answered, **"Why did you call me good? There is none good but one, that is, God."** (Matt. 19:17) If this was the case, how could he accept that someone call him God in reality?

Regarding Psalms (110:1), it did not mean Jesus (PBUH) in any way, but it meant the expected messiah whom the Jews were awaiting, and he is the Prophet Mohammad (PBUH).

Peter made a mistake when considering the passage as it was for Jesus (PBUH), he said, **"For David did not ascend into the heavens, but he himself says, '"The Lord said to my Lord, Sit at my right hand, until I make your enemies your footstool.' Let all the house of Israel; therefore, know for certain that God has made him both Lord and Christ, this**

Jesus whom you crucified." Now when they heard this they were cut to the heart.” (Acts: 2:34-37)

The proof of Peter's misunderstanding, and the Christians after him, was that Jesus (PBUH) denied that he was the expected messiah, whom David mentioned. **“While the Pharisees were gathered together, Jesus asked them a question, saying, What do you think about the Christ?** (Whom the Jews were awaiting) **Whose son is he? They said to him, The Son of David. He said to them, how is it then that David, in spirit, called him Lord, saying, The LORD said to my Lord, Sit on my right hand, till I make your enemies your footstool? If David then calls him Lord, how is he his son? And no man was able to answer him a word, nor from that day anyone dare to ask him any more questions.”** (Matt. 22:41-46)

Jesus (PBUH) asked the Jews about the expected messiah who David and other prophets had prophesized. **“What do you think about the Christ? Whose son is he? They said to him, The Son of David.”** He showed them that they were wrong and said, **“If David then calls him Lord, how is he his son?”**

Mark also mentioned it, **“"How can the scribes say that the Christ is the son of David? David himself, in the Holy Spirit, declared, "'The Lord said to my Lord, Sit at my right hand, until I put your enemies under your feet.' David himself calls him Lord. So how is he his son?** (Mark12: 35-37)

We also find the same in Luke. **"How can they say that the Christ is David's son? For David himself says in the Book of Psalms, "'The Lord said to my Lord, Sit at my right hand, until I make your enemies your footstool.' David thus calls him Lord, so how is he his son?"** (Luke 20:40-44)

The expected messiah is not a descendant of David, and Christians believe that Jesus (PBUH) is from David's offspring as recorded in his genealogy in Matthew and Luke. Does Priest Ibrahim Saeed still insist in considering us as illiterates and unreasonable contenders because we say that that passage was not for Jesus (PBUH)?

What came in Isaiah regarding Emanuel was not for Jesus (PBUH) either, for that was never his name, and no one had ever called him that. The story in the Book of Isaiah speaks about an event, which happened centuries before Jesus (PBUH), when Rosin, the King of

Edom, conspired with Faqah ben Ramlia, the King of the Northern Israelite Kingdom, against the Southern Kingdom and its King Ahaz.

The birth of Emanuel was Allah's (S.W) sign of the end of punishment on Judea's Kingdom, the destruction of Rosin's and Faqah's Kingdoms, and the death of the two kings by the hands of the Assyrians.

Isaiah says, **"Again the LORD spoke to Ahaz... Therefore, the Lord himself will give you a sign. Behold, the virgin shall conceive and bear a son, and shall call his name Immanuel. He shall eat curds and honey. when he knows how to refuse the evil and choose the good. For before the boy knows how to refuse the evil and choose the good, the land whose two kings you dread will be deserted. The LORD will bring upon you and upon your people and upon your father's house such days as have not come since the day that Ephraim departed from Judah--the king of Assyria." In that day the LORD will whistle for the fly that is at the end of the streams of Egypt, and for the bee that is in the land of Assyria. "** (Isaiah 7:10 – 18)

"Then the LORD said to me, "Take a large tablet and write on with the pen of man, 'for Maher-shalal-hashbaz.'... and she conceived and bore a son. Then the LORD said to me, "Call his name Maher-shalal-hashbaz; for before the boy knows how to cry 'My father' or 'My mother,' the wealth of Damascus and the spoil of Samaria will be carried away before the king of Assyria."" (Isaiah 8:1- 4)

It is clear that this passage is about the Assyrian invasion of Palestine, which happened centuries before Jesus (PBUH). During that time, the boy was born, his father gave him a name after King Ahaz's victory, which is **"Mahershalalhashbaz"**, and that name means, "Dashing to pillage and robbery" "Because God is with him".

This prophecy came true, and King Ahaz had his victory when the Assyrian king came and captured the two conspiring kings. **"The LORD spoke to me again: ... therefore, behold, the Lord is bringing up against them the waters of the River, mighty and many, the king of Assyria and all his glory. And it will rise over all its channels and go over all its banks, and it will sweep on into Judah, it will overflow and pass on, reaching even to the neck, and its outspread wings will fill**

the breadth of your land, O Immanuel." Be broken, you peoples, and be shattered; give ear, all you far countries; strap on your armor and be shattered. Take counsel together, but it will come to nothing; speak a word, but it will not stand, for God is with us. " (Isaiah: 8: 5-10)

I have to mention here, that Luke's author used a fabricated passage from the Book of Isaiah. Neither in the old Hebrew originals, nor in the Torah's old translation, have we found any trace of the word "betolah", that means, "virgin", which was invented and fabricated by the Seventieth Translation writers, and the evangelists copied it from them after that, for it suited them.

The word in the old Torah's translations such as ecoela, thehodoshen, and semix translations, which belong to the second century, is "Alma" which means, "Young woman".[1] In the Revised Standard Version, 1952, the editors had changed the word "Virgin" into "Young woman", but only in the English translation.[2]

None of the names, which are in the passage in Isaiah (Isaiah 9:6), were names for Jesus (PBUH). **"For to us a child is born, to us a son is given: and the government shall be upon his shoulder: and his name shall be called Wonderful, Counselor, The mighty God, The everlasting Father, the Prince of Peace."** (Isaiah 9:6)

Where and when did any one call him wonderful, counselor, the mighty, the everlasting Father, or the Prince of Peace? There is not a single passage in the entire Bible that can show proof of that.

If the Christians say that these were characteristics of Jesus (PBUH) and not names, we also say that these titles were not for him in any way. These characteristics speak of a victorious king who will rule his people and inherit David's kingdom, and that is too far from Jesus (PBUH) according to the facts and the Gospels' passages. Jesus (PBUH) was never a King of his people even for a day. On the contrary, he was a fugitive, scared and worried of the Jews; he also fled when his people wanted to make him a king. **"Perceiving then that they were about to come and take him by force to make him king, Jesus withdrew again to the mountain by himself."** (John 6:15)

---

[1] - An Introduction to the Old Testament, Dr. Samuel Yosof, pp 260

[2] - The History of Christian Ideology, Hanna Jerjes ElKhodary, Vol.1 pp 175. Is the Holy Bible God's word? , Ahmad Deedat, pp 24-25.

He fled because his kingdom was not of this world and not on the throne of David, but was a spiritual kingdom in the hereafter. **"Jesus answered, "My kingdom doesn't belong to this world. If it did, my followers would have fought to keep me from being handed over to the Jewish leaders. No, my kingdom doesn't belong to this world." "** (John 18:36)

In addition, Isaiah talked about the Prince of Peace and that cannot be an attribution to Jesus (PBUH), because the Gospels mentioned the opposite about him. **"Do not think that I have come to bring peace to the earth. I have not come to bring peace, but a sword. For I have come to set a man against his father, and a daughter against her mother, and a daughter-in-law against her mother-in-law. And a person's enemies will be those of his own household."** (Matt.10:34-36) Could this Gospels' Jesus be a prince of peace?

Furthermore, Isaiah talked about a capable person, he did not talk about an incapable one, who cannot do anything by himself. **"I can do nothing on my own: as I hear, I judge"** (John 5:30)

""Truly, truly, I say to you, the Son can do nothing of his own accord, but only what he sees the Father doing. For whatever the Father does, that the Son does likewise. " (John 5:19)

THE USE OF THE DIVINITY AND LORDSHIP TERMS IN THE BIBLE

Calling Jesus (PBUH), "lord" or "god" is not evidence of his divinity, for they are commonly in use in the Holy Bible. The Holy Bible uses these two words to name many creatures, among them are the angels.

In the Book of Judges, we read, **"The angel of the LORD appeared no more to Manoah and to his wife. Then Manoah knew that he was the angel of the LORD. And Manoah said to his wife, "We shall surely die, for we have seen God." "** (Judges 13:21-22) (ESV), but he meant "the angel of Allah (S.W)".

Allah's (S.W) angel appeared to Sarah and gave her good news about Isaac. **"And the angel of the LORD said to her... she called the name of the LORD that spoke to her, 'you are the God of seeing.'** (Gen. 16:11-13)

Another example is in the Book of Exodus, which talks about the angel who accompanied the Israelites when they departed from Egypt and the passage calls him god. **"And the LORD went before them by day in a pillar of a cloud, to lead them along the way; and by night in a pillar of fire, to give them light; that they might travel by day and night.... And the angel of God, which went before the camp of Israel, removed and went behind them; and the pillar of the cloud went from before their face, and stood behind them."** (Ex.13:21, 14:19)

The Torah also gives these names to some prophets, but it does not mean the real meaning of the word. Allah (S.W) spoke to Moses regarding Aaron (PBUT), **"He will be to you as a mouth and you will be to him as God."** (Ex.4:16) (ESV), **"And the LORD said to Moses, see, I have made you a god to Pharaoh: and Aaron your brother shall be your prophet."** (Ex. 7:1)

The prophets named Gods in the Torah metaphorically, and it meant "messengers of God", as mentioned in the First Book of Samuel, **"(Formerly in Israel, when a man went to inquire of God, he said, "Come, let us go to the seer," for today's "prophet" was formerly called a seer.) "** (Sam.1 9:9)

The Torah also mentions the word "God" and it refers to Judges, because they Judge according to Allah's (S.W) Law. **"But if the servant shall plainly say... then his master shall bring him to God, and shall bring him to the door."**(Ex.21:5-6)

In the next chapter of the same book, we read, **"If the thief is not found, the owner of the house shall come near to God to show whether or not he has put his hand to his neighbor's property... The one whom God condemns shall pay double to his neighbor."** (Ex.22: 8-9)

In the Book of Deuteronomy, we read, **"then both parties to the dispute shall appear before the LORD, before the priests"** (Duet. 19:17)

In the Book of Psalms, **"God stands in the congregation of God; He judges among the gods. How long will you judge unjustly, and respect the persons of the wicked?"**(Psalms 82:1) It is clear that this passage talks about the Judges and the noble Israelites.

The use of this word has spread even further to call all the Israelites, as mentioned in Psalms. **"I said, you are gods, and all of you sons of the Most High. Nevertheless you shall die like men."** (Psalms 82:6) This passage is what Jesus (PBUH) quoted while he was speaking to the Jews. **"Jesus answered them, Is it not written in your law, I said, you are gods? If he called them gods, to whom the word of God came, and the scripture cannot be broken; Say you of him, whom the Father has sanctified, and sent to the world, you blasphemes; because I said, I am the Son of God?"** (John 10:34)

The Holy Books continue in giving these names even to devils and nations' false gods. Not only that Paul called the devil god, but also the belly. He said about the devil: **"In whom the god of this world had blinded the minds of them which believe not, lest the light of the glorious gospel of Christ."** (Cor.2 4:4)

He said the following about people who follow their desires: **"whose God is their belly, and whose glory is in their shame."** (Phi. 3:19)

We find the same thing in Psalms. **"For I know that the LORD is great, and that our Lord is above all gods."** (Psalms 135:5).

The divinity of the belly and the others is metaphoric and not real.

In "Explanation of the Faith's principles" the authors wrote, "Moses was called god by God himself as he was acting on God's behalf, and not because he was divine. The same goes for the Judges because they judge according to God's Law. The belly, the statues and the money, it was called as such because some people had taken it as gods, and the devil was called god because he controls our world".[1]

This is the Holy Bible's language and way of expression; whoever insists on taking its words literally, is wrong. The lordship mentioned above was just metaphoric, and the same goes for Jesus (PBUH).

In his book "the Precious Holy Bible seekers' guide", Dr. Samaan Kahloon wrote, "Expressions in the Holy Bible are very metaphoric and mysterious especially in the Old Testament".

He also wrote, "Expressions in the New Testament are also very metaphoric, specially "the words of our Savior", and because some of the Christian teachers used literal interpretation methods, many of the false and corrupted opinions were spread around..."[2]

In addition, when Jesus (PBUH) heard about these metaphoric gods, he declared that there is only One True God who is Allah (S.W), he said, **"And this is eternal life, that they know you the only true God, and Jesus Christ whom you have sent."** (John 17:3) which clearly means that heaven and eternal life will be obtained by bearing witness that Allah (S.W) is One, and that Jesus (PBUH) is his messenger, and this is what all Muslims believe.

---

[1] Explanation of the Essence of Faith, Dr. Priest Andrew Watson, and Dr. Priest Ibrahim Saeed, pp 44

[2] The Truth Revealed, Rahamtu Allah Al-Hindi Vol.3 pp 702.

2- VERSES ATTRIBUTING DIVINE SON-SHIP TO JESUS (PBUH)

The Gospels speak of Jesus (PBUH) as the Son of God, and Christians consider that as evidence of his divinity. Is that consideration correct, and what is the meaning of "the Son of God"?

Did Jesus (PBUH) call himself the "Son of God"?

The first issue that we have to consider is that Jesus (PBUH) did not call himself "the Son of God" except once (John 10:36). The rest of the Gospels' passages tell us that his disciples and his contemporaries also said so. This is what made some scholars doubt that Jesus (PBUH) or his disciples had truly uttered these words.[1]

In his book, "The Gospel Dictionary", Senger wrote, "That Jesus himself used this term is uncertain". In this regard, Charles Gene Pair said, "The firm conclusion of the researchers' studies is, that Jesus never claimed that he was the expected messiah, and he never called himself the Son of God... for this language was not in use except by Christians who were influenced by the Greek Culture."[2]

Coleman, the prominent scholar, said regarding this title, "The disciples, mentioned in Acts, were influenced by their master who did not use this title and he did not want it, and then they followed his steps".

---

[1] - In this regard, Pfleiderer, the prominent German scholar, said in his book on early Christianity, "in the stories of the apostles as in all the secular historians of antiquity these speeches are free compositions, in which the author has his heroes speak in the way that he himself thinks they could have spoken in the given situation" (p.500f.) (Kautsky, Karl, Foundations of Christianity, 1908, pp 22)

In his book, " Saint Mark", Nineham said, "Anyone who has looked critically at the various modern 'lives' of Jesus, with their widely different pictures of him, will realize how largely their authors have had to draw on their own imaginations." (Nineham, D.E, Saint Mark, 1963, pp 35)

(This footnote was added by the proofreader, and it was taken from his book, "Contemporary Christianity Under The Light of Science and Reason" p 44, 61)

[2] - Christianity, its beginning and its development, Charles Gene Pier, pp 50

Jesus (PBUH) is also the "Son of Man"

There are eighty-three passages in the Gospels, which mention that people repeatedly call Jesus (PBUH) "the Son of Man", and these passages contradict and refute the few passages that call him (PBUH) the "Son of God".

Jesus (PBUH), according to the Egyptian Christian scholar Matta El Meskeen, had given himself this title "in order to hide his true divine son-ship when he spoke about himself".[1]

If these passages, which call Jesus (PBUH) "the Son of God", are proof of his divinity, the other passages, which call him "the Son of Man", are solid proof of his humanity, dismissing the divinity passages to their metaphoric meaning.

In Matthew, we read the following, **"And Jesus said to him, the foxes have holes, and the birds of the air have nests; but the Son of man has nowhere to lay his head."** (Matt. 8:20)

In Mark, **"The Son of man indeed goes, as it is written of him"** (Mark 14:21)

The Torah mentions that, **"God is not a man that he should lie; neither the son of man that he should repent"** (Numbers 23:9) therefore, Jesus (PBUH) is not God.

There are many sons of God in the Bible, are they all Gods?

The title "Son of God", which was attributed to Jesus (PBUH), was attributed to many others, and they were not considered as gods. However, their son-ship was metaphoric, meaning, believers and righteous. According to the Bible, the following people are sons of God:

---

[1]- The Gospel according to Matthew's commentary, Father Matta El Meskeen, pp 147. Why did Jesus (PBUH) hide this issue, why did not he face us with his identity, why did he hide his claimed divinity with this title, which cries loud in the face of those who claim his divinity, that he is a man and a son of man!

Adam was the Son of God. **"Adam, which was the son of God."**(Luke 3:38)

David was the Son of God. **"I will declare the decree: the LORD has said to me, you art my Son; this day have I begotten you."** (Psalms 2:7)

Solomon was the Son of God. **"He shall build me a house, and I will establish his throne for ever. I will be his father, and he shall be my son"** (Chro.1 17:12-13)

The writer of Luke gave this title to the angels, because the use of it was common. **"For they are equal to the angels; and are the children of God."** (Luke 20:36)

Other passages named others as sons of God or that God is their father. The disciples were sons of God, but no Christian said that they were Gods. **"But go to my brethren, and say to them, I ascend to my Father, and your Father; and to my God, and your God."** (John 20:17) **"Be ye therefore perfect, even as your Father which is in heaven is perfect."** (Matt. 5:48)

The entire Jewish race is also the Children of God. **"They said to him, "We were not born of sexual immorality. We have one Father--even God." "** (John 8:41)

What come in Psalms and Job are alike. **"For who in the heaven can be compared unto the LORD? Who among the sons of the mighty can be likened unto the LORD?"** (Psalms 89:6)

"Now there was a day when the sons of God came to present themselves before the LORD." (Job 1:6)

We also see that the Torah had given this title to the strong and noble people, and no Christian or others considered them as Gods. **"The sons of God saw that the daughters of man were attractive. And they took as their wives any they chose. when the sons of God came in to the daughters of man and they bore children to them. These were the mighty men who were of old, the men of renown. "** (Gen. 6:2 - 4)

Therefore, Christians cannot take these passages as evidence of Jesus' (PBUH) divinity, and prevent using the same for Adam,

Solomon and the others. In order to do so, they have to present solid predominant evidence, which they do not and will never be able to have.

When the Jews wanted to fabricate an accusation for Jesus (PBUH), they said that he blasphemed by saying that he was the Son of God and meaning it in reality. Jesus (PBUH) rebuked them, and explained that it was metaphoric and not reality, as used in their books, which made all of the Jews sons of God.

He (PBUH) said, **"If he called them gods, unto whom the word of God came, and the scripture cannot be broken; Say ye of him, whom the Father hath sanctified, and sent into the world, Thou blasphemes; because I said, I am the Son of God? If I do not the works of my Father, believe me not."** (John 10: 35-37), meaning, if your book called you "sons of God" metaphorically, me too, I am saying that we are equal and I am the "son of God" metaphorically.

The Correct Meaning of "Son-ship"

The meaning of the son-ship of Jesus (PBUH) and others has a figurative and metaphoric meaning, which are, the one who is dear to God, the one who is obedient to God or the one who believes in God.

Mark, when he spoke about the centurion, who saw the crucified person, wrote, **"And when the centurion, whom stood over against him, saw that he so cried out, and gave up the ghost, he said, truly this man was the Son of God."** (Mark 15:39)

When Luke mentioned the event, he changed the sentence to its equal. He says, **"Now when the centurion saw what was done, he glorified God, saying, certainly this was a righteous man."** (Luke 23:47)

We find the same use of this meaning in the Gospel according to John when he spoke about the believers. He said, **"But as many as received him, to them gave he power to become the sons of God, *even* to them that believe on his name."** (John 1:12) and he said, **"He that is of God hears God's words"** (John 8:47)
Paul declared the same fact, he said, **"For as many as are led by the Spirit of God, they are the sons of God."** (Rom. 8:14)

This metaphoric use is common in the Holy Books that speak about the children of evil and the children of the world. (John 8:44) (Luke 16:8).

When the devils mentioned the real meaning of the son-ship to Jesus (PBUH), he condemned them. **"And devils also came out of many, crying out, and saying, Thou art Christ the Son of God. And he rebuked *them* suffered them not to speak: for they knew that he was Christ."** (Luke 4:41) He is the Christ only and not a real Son of God.

Did Jesus (PBUH) claim that he is a real son of Allah (S.W) and he is equal to Him?

One of the Christians' allegations of Christ's (PBUH) divinity is that he declared that he is equal to Allah (S.W) considering what came in the Gospel according to John. **"Therefore the Jews sought the more to kill him, because he not only had broken the Sabbath, but said also that God was his Father, making himself equal with God."** (John 5:18) No doubt, that reading this passage out of context would make it evidence that indicates Jesus' (PBUH) declaration of his real son-ship to God. This, only the unknowledgeable and ignorant people can accept, for, it is not true.

To understand this passage, we have to read it in context. Jesus (PBUH) had treated an ill person on the Sabbath, which the Jews considered wrong; therefore, **"the Jews persecuted Jesus, and sought to slay him, because he had done these things on the Sabbath day."** (John 5:16) but he explained to them why he had done so. **"But Jesus answered them, My Father worked hitherto, and I work."** (John 5:17), which means that, as God works on all days, I am also doing a good deed.

The Jews, who wanted to create a problem with Jesus (PBUH), considered his words "My father worked" as praising himself and a claim of the real son-ship to God. They considered this son-ship, which they commonly used metaphorically, as blasphemy and it meant that he was making himself equal to Allah (S.W); therefore, increased their desire to kill him. **"Therefore the Jews sought the more to kill him, because he not only had broken the Sabbath, but said also that God was his Father, making himself equal with God."** (John 5:18)

With a long meaningful speech, Jesus (PBUH) answered them, explaining and refuting their claim, and proving to Christians their incorrect understanding. (John 5:19 -47) I will summarize these meaningful points according to their subject.

1- Jesus (PBUH) assured all that he was following Allah's (S.W) path when he worked on the Sabbath, for he did not do something but what agrees with Allah's (S.W) statute. **"Then answered Jesus and said unto them, Verily, verily, I say unto you, The Son can do nothing of himself, but what he see the Father do: for what things so ever he doeth, these also doeth the Son likewise."** (John 5:19)

2- He spoke about many great things that Allah (S.W) has given him, **"For as the Father raised up the dead, and quicken them; even so the Son quicken whom he will. For the Father judges no man, but hath committed all judgment unto the Son... For as the Father hath life in himself; so hath he given to the Son to have life in himself; And hath given him authority to execute judgment also."** (John 5: 21- 27), but all these gifts, were from Allah (S.W), and that did not mean that Jesus (PBUH) is Allah (S.W), for Allah (S.W) can do all that Himself without needing any one to give Him anything.

Jesus (PBUH) had clarified why he did so. It was because Allah (S.W) has given him these things considering his humanity and not divinity. He says, **"And hath given him authority to execute judgment also, because he is the Son of man."** (John 5: 27)

He affirmed that he had no authority by himself, and he could not do any thing except what Allah (S.W) permitted him to do. **"I can of mine own self do nothing: as I hear, I judge: and my judgment is just; because I seek not mine own will, but the will of the Father which hath sent me."** (John 5: 30) That is to prove that he is the son of man, not the Son of Allah (S.W) in reality, or the second hypostasis in Trinity as the Church's Councils claimed.

The great miracles that Allah (S.W) gave to Jesus (PBUH) were for two reasons. The first, is as he (PBUH) said, **"For the Father loves the Son, and shows him all things that himself doeth".** The second is to prove his prophet-hood and make the people believe in him. **"And he will show him greater works than these that ye may marvel. That all men should honour the**

Son, even as they honour the Father. He that honoureth not the Son honoureth not the Father which hath sent him... for the works which the Father hath given me to finish, the same works that I do, bear witness of me, that the Father hath sent me." (John5:20, 23, 36)

3- Jesus (PBUH) assured that Allah (S.W) confirms his honesty. He said, **"If I bear witness of myself, my witness is not true. There is another that beareth witness of me; and I know that the witness which he witnesseth of me is true... And the Father himself, which hath sent me, hath borne witness of me. Ye have neither heard his voice at any time, nor seen his shape."** (John 5:31, 37)

The record of this testimony is in the previous sacred books that foretold about him. **"Search the scriptures; for in them ye think ye have eternal life: and they are they which testify of me... For had ye believed Moses, ye would have believed me: for he wrote of me."** (John5:39, 46)

Moses' (PBUH) books, which Jesus (PBUH) and the Jews accept, do not contain a line regarding any prophecy about an incarnated or crucified God. They testify the coming of a noble prophet. Do the Christians not claim that Moses had prophesized Jesus (PBUT) when he said, **"I will raise them up a Prophet from among their brethren, like unto thee?** (Deut. 18:18)

One of the people, who testify for Jesus (PBUH), is John the Baptist (PBUH). However, Jesus (PBUH) dispensed this true testimony with Allah's (S.W) one-ness, which is in their scriptures. **"Ye sent unto John, and he bore witness unto the truth. But I receive not testimony from man... But I have greater witness than that of John"** (John 5:33, 36)

There is nothing in the Baptist's (PBUH) words that conveys the divinity of Christ, for he sent his disciples to ask Jesus (PBUH) whether he was the expected prophet or not. (Matt. 11:3)

4- Jesus (PBUH) declared that there was a difference between him and Allah (S.W) when he said, **"For the Father loves the Son, and shows him all things that himself doeth...There is another that beareth witness of me... And the Father himself, which hath sent me, hath borne witness of me... Do**

not think that I will accuse you to the Father". (John5:20, 32, 37, 45) All these prove that Jesus (PBUH) is not Allah (S.W), for the lover is unlike the beloved, the witness is unlike the one who witnessed for, the sender is unlike the consignee, and the complainant is unlike the judge.

5- Jesus (PBUH) told the Jews that the way to eternal life is to believe in him and in his words. **"Verily, verily, I say unto you, He that heareth my word, and believeth on him that sent me, hath everlasting life, and shall not come into condemnation; but is passed from death unto life."** (John 5:24)

Those who did not believe in him will face as he said. **"And ye will not come to me, that ye might have life. I receive not honour from men. But I know you, that ye have not the love of God in you. I am come in my Father's name, and ye receive me not: if another shall come in his own name, him ye will receive. How can ye believe, which receive honour one of another, and seek not the honour that cometh from God only?** (John 5:40 - 44)

From the above mentioned, we have seen that Jesus (PBUH) did not claim that he was equal to Allah (S.W), neither did he claim that the authority he had was his own, but he declared that Allah (S.W) had honored him and given it to him.

The Son Who Was Descended from Heaven

Christians believe that we should distinguish the son-ship of Jesus (PBUH) from the son-ship of the others. They do not argue that the passages, which mentioned the son-ship of others, are metaphoric, but Jesus (PBUH) is the Son of God in reality, for he is the only son who is descendant from above or from heaven. **"He that cometh from above is above all."** (John 3:31)

They believe that the sign of his divinity shines in his saying, **"Ye are from beneath; I am from above: ye are of this world; I am not of this world.** (John 8:23) and that shows, according to Christians, that he is a unique divine son unlike the other sons.

The meaning of this heavenly descending is the descending of the signs and the statutes, and not the descending of the person himself and that makes him equal to all prophets. John the Baptist (PBUH) is one of them. Jesus (PBUH) asked the Jews, saying, **"The baptism of John, whence was it? From heaven, or of men? And they reasoned with themselves, saying, If we shall say, From heaven; he will say unto us, Why did ye not then believe him? But if we shall say, of men; we fear the people."** (Matt. 21:25-26)

I need to mention also that there are many true heavenly descendants in the Bible, but Christians do not consider them gods.

The angel of Allah (S.W) was descended from heaven. **"And, behold, there was a great earthquake: for the angel of the Lord descended from heaven."** (Matt. 28:2)

The disciples were also descendants from above or from Allah (S.W), as mentioned in the Gospels, which means they believe in his name. **"But as many as received him, to them gave he power to become the sons of God, even to them that believe on his name."** (John 1:12). This is a spiritual birth, which gives the heart of the sinner a great, complete and continuous change, as he or she is born again, and this happens when he or she believes and repents.

The believers in Jesus (PBUH) are born from above by the faith that Allah (S.W) has given them. They are alike with other believers, as Jesus (PBUH) said, **"Truly, truly I tell you, unless a person is born from above he cannot see the kingdom of God."** (John 3:3), **"Whosoever believeth that Jesus is the Christ, is born of God."** (John1 5:1), and **"that every one that doeth righteousness is born of him."** (John1 2:29)

Jesus' (PBUH) saying, **"I am not of this world"**, is not a proof of his divinity in any way, for he meant that he is different from other humans by refusing this secular world, for which other people are longing.

He (PBUH) said the same about his disciples when he felt that they wanted the eternal life, leaving this secular world. **"If ye were of the world, the world would love his own: but because ye are not of the world, but I have chosen you out of the world, therefore the world hates you."** (John 15:19)

In another passage, he said, **"I have given them thy word; and the world hath hated them, because they are not of the world, even as I am not of the world."** (John 17:14),

He (PBUH) said about his disciples what he said of himself, they were not of this world. If those words could make him God, it should also make all the disciples gods as well, but his expression was metaphoric as if we say, "this person is not from this world" and we mean, that he or she do not desire this materialistic world, but seeking Allah's (S.W) love and the eternal life in the hereafter.

3- VERSES OF THE DIVINE INCARNATION IN JESUS (PBUH)

Christians believe that some of the Holy passages convey divine incarnation in Jesus (PBUH). The following are some of these passages:

"That ye may know, and believe, that the Father is in me, and I in him." (John 10:38), **"He that hath seen me hath seen the Father... I am in the Father, and the Father in me."** (John 14:9-10)

His saying, **"I and the father are one"** (John 10:30), remains the strongest evidence that Christians present to prove the divinity of Christ (PBUH). These passages, according to Christians, declare that Jesus (PBUH) is Allah (S.W) himself, and that Allah (S.W) is incarnated in him.

God's Metaphoric Incarnation in His Creations

Scholars have analyzed these passages and proved the Christians' misunderstanding of them. The Christians' understanding of the verses that contain Allah's (S.W) incarnation in Jesus (PBUH) - as they understand - is wrong. It is an indisputable fact that Allah's (S.W) incarnation in his creations is a metaphorical incarnation, and it is the same for Jesus (PBUH).

Allah (S.W), according to the Holy Bible, incarnates in many, which means the divine gifts (or attributes) are incarnated and not Allah (S.W) himself. In the First Epistle of John we read, **"Whosoever shall confess that Jesus is the Son of God, God dwelled in him, and he in God. And we have known and believed the love that God hath to us. God is love; and he that dwelled in love dwelled in God and God in him."** (John (1) 4:15-16). Therefore, Allah's (S.W) incarnation or dwelling in those who believe in Jesus (PBUH), is not a true self-incarnation, otherwise, they will all be Gods.

In addition, Allah (S.W) incarnates or dwells in anyone who keeps the commandments, but that does not mean that that person becomes God. **"And he that kept his commandments dwelled in him, and he in him. And hereby we know that he abided in us, by the Spirit which he hath given us."** (John (1) 3:24). The meaning here is that Allah's (S.W) guidance and support are with and upon them.

sake, and this, we find in the same Epistle. **"No man hath seen God at any time. If we love one another, God dwelleth in us, and his love is perfected in us. Hereby know we that we dwell in him, and he in us, because He hath given us of His Spirit."** (John (1) 4:12-13). The same is in the Gospel according to John. **"I in them and you in me"** (John 17:23)

These verses denote and imply divine incarnation in all believers; it is, without doubt, a metaphorical incarnation, therefore, it is the same for Jesus (PBUH), and if some one wishes to claim otherwise, he or she should present the evidence.

Furthermore, the Torah mentions a real incarnation of Allah (S.W) in his creations, but Christians do not consider them gods.

In Exodus we read, **"In the place, O LORD, which thou hast made for thee to dwell in."** (Exodus 15:17) and in Psalms, **"Why leap ye, ye high hills? This is the hill which God desires to dwell in; yea, the LORD will dwell in it for ever."** (Psalms 68:16), and no one worships that mountain.

There are two important claimed incarnation passages, which are, (John 10:30), and (John 14:9), do these two verses prove Jesus' (PBUH) divinity?

A) **"I and the father are one"** (John 10:30)

This sentence, which is attributed to Jesus (PBUH), is one important verse for those who believe in Jesus' divinity. They understand that there is a real unity between him and Allah (S.W), which he (PBUH) himself had declared in front of the Jews and, that he meant his divinity.

In order to understand this passage, we have to read it from the beginning. During the Feast of Dedication, Jesus (PBUH) was walking in Solomon's porch, the Jews came and said, **"How long dost thou make us to doubt? If thou be the Christ, tell us plainly. Jesus answered them, I told you, and ye believed not: the works that I do in my Father's name, they bear witness of me. But ye believe not, because ye are not of my sheep, as I said unto you. My sheep hear my voice, and I know them, and they follow me: And I give unto them**

eternal life; and they shall never perish, neither shall any man pluck them out of my hand. My Father, which gave them me, is greater than all; and no man is able to pluck them out of my Father's hand. I and my Father are one."
(John 10:24-30)

The passage from the beginning talks about a metaphoric issue.[1] His sheep, which means his disciples, will follow him, so he will give them eternal life, which is heaven, and no one will take his sheep away from him, which means from his way and guidance, for, Allah (S.W) has given him and no one can take that from Allah (S.W), who is the greatest. Allah (S.W) and Jesus (PBUH) want good for these sheep; thus, the unity is of the objective and not the essence.

The Jews in Solomon's porch misunderstood Jesus' (PBUH) words, exactly, like the Christian's, therefore, **'the Jews took up stones again to stone him...For a good work we stone thee not; but for blasphemy; and because that thou, being a man, makest thyself God.**

Jesus (PBUH) realized their misunderstanding, and was surprised how they could misunderstand his words since they are well acquainted with the Bible's metaphoric language.

Quoting what comes in Psalms 82:6, he answered them, **'Is it not written in your law, I said, Ye are gods?'** He meant that, how could you be surprised with my words since it is common in your book, which made all Israelites gods metaphorically? Therefore, Jesus (PBUH) deserves being a metaphoric god, more than all the Israelites. **'If he called them gods, unto whom the word of God came...Say ye of him, whom the Father hath sanctified, and sent into the world, Thou blasphemest; because I said, I am the Son of God? If I do not the works of my Father, believe me not.** (John 10:35-37)

Giving his opinion about this passage, Matta El Meskeen said, "Jesus quoted Psalm 82, for God's angel gives this attribute to the council that gathered to judge according to God's word... and that is an answer to their claim, which considered Jesus as committing

---

[1] Priest James Anis concludes that one has to explain the verses metaphorically if the chapter is full of metaphoric, which one cannot explain it literally. How about this verse that is metaphoric? (see Methodical Divinity Science, James Anis, pp 713)

blasphemy, while all those who received God's words are considered in the Torah as gods."[1]

Therefore, with this verse from Psalms, Jesus (PBUH) corrected the Jews' and the Christians' misunderstanding about his unity with Allah (S.W).

This way of expression about the similarity of will and objective, is common in the Christians' sacred writings, especially in the Gospel according to John. Quoting Jesus, about the disciples, John said, **'That they all may be one; as thou, Father, art in me, and I in thee, that they** (the disciples) **also may be one in us that they may be one, even as we are one: I in them, and thou in me'** (John 17:20-23). This dwelling and incarnation are metaphoric; otherwise, we should consider the disciples as gods.

The passage uses the word "as", which denotes similarity between the two parties, and the meaning is, (as Jesus and the father are one, also the disciples, Jesus and the father are one), meaning, similar in objective, and not self-similarity, for no Christian speaks of a real self unity of Jesus and his disciples.

In another passage, Jesus (PBUH) mentioned the same meaning. He said about the disciples, **'Holy Father, keep through your own name those whom thou hast given me, that they may be one, as we are.** (John 17:11). That means as our unity is an objective unity; therefore, their unity should be like ours as well.

Similarly, a verse comes in another chapter. **'At that day ye shall know that I am in my Father, and ye in me, and I in you.** (John 14:20).

Paul said the same, **'For ye are the temple of the living God; as God hath said, I will dwell in them, and walk in them; and I will be their God, and they shall be my people.'** (Co. (2) 6:16). Again, Paul said, **'I have planted, Apollos watered... Now he that plants and he that waters are one... For we are laborers together with God'** (Co.1 3:6-9). Paul's unity with Apollo, is also the shared objective unity.

---

[1] -The Gospel according to John, Priest Matta Almeskeen, Vol. 1, pp 643-644

Describing the relationship between husband and wife, the Torah says, **'therefore, shall a man leave his father and his mother, and shall cleave unto his wife: and they shall be one flesh.'** (Gen. 2:24). Means they are the same, not because their two bodies became one body.

Therefore, we should not understand these verses shallowly and literally, as Matthew said, **'And said, for this cause shall a man leave father and mother, and shall cleave to his wife: and they twain shall be one flesh?'** (Matt. 19:5). The same is for Jesus (PBUH) when he said, **"I and the father are one"**.

The Quran mentions the same about Prophet Mohammad (PBUH), but the Muslims do not understand or take it as real God incarnation in Mohammad (PBUH). **"Verily those who plight their fealty to thee do no less than plight their fealty to God."** (Holy Quran 48:10)

No Muslim said, or will say, that Allah (S.W) and His Prophet Mohammad (PBUH) are one self, unlike what Christians say regarding Jesus' (PBUH) saying, **"I and the father are one"**.

B) Jesus saying, who has seen me, has seen the Father.

Another important passage for Christians, which they consider as evidence of Jesus' (PBUH) divinity, is what we find in the Gospel according to John, **"Whoever has seen me has seen the Father"** (John 14:9). They understand that the father is Jesus, and seeing Jesus is in fact seeing Allah (S.W).

This shallow understanding is poor, faulty and feeble, and creates many problems that suggest blasphemy to Allah (S.W), who is above all problems and any human faults. If seeing Jesus (PBUH) is considered as seeing the Father, it is compulsory to consider slapping Jesus and spitting in his face (Matt. 27:30) as slapping and spitting on the Father Himself, Allah (S.W), Creator of the heavens and earth.

Similarly, Jesus' ignorance of the Day of Judgment is considered as a nescience to Allah (S.W) (Mark 13:32-33). When Jesus ate and

drank (Luke 24:42-43) it was also considered, according to this shallow understanding, food and drink for the Father.
Can anyone imagine that Allah (S.W), who created everything, eats, drinks, micturates, and defecates?

To understand the passage correctly, we read from the beginning, and it says, **"I go to prepare a place for you. And if I go and prepare a place for you, I will come again, and receive you to myself"**, the place that he mentioned is the kingdom. Thomas did not understand and said, **"Lord, we do not know where you are going. How can we know the way?"** (John 14:5).

He understood that Jesus (PBUH) spoke about a real road and a real journey. Correcting him and explaining that it is a spiritual journey, Jesus (PBUH) said, **"I am the way, the truth, and the life"**, meaning, following God's statute and His religion alone will lead to the kingdom of heaven.

Then, Philip asked him to show them Allah (S.W); thus, Jesus (PBUH) scolded him, saying, **"Have I been with you so long, and you still do not know me, Philip? Whoever has seen me has seen the Father. How can you say, 'Show us the Father'?**
 (John 14:10) meaning, how could you ask such a thing, since you are a Jew, and you know that Allah (S.W) cannot be seen? Who ever has seen me, has seen the Father, when he witnessed Allah's deeds – the miracles –, which I performed.

This passage is the same as in Matthew, **"Then the King will say to those on his right, 'Come, you who are blessed by my Father, inherit the kingdom prepared for you from the foundation of the world. For I was hungry and you gave me food, I was thirsty and you gave me drink, I was a stranger and you welcomed me, I was naked and you clothed me, I was sick and you visited me, I was in prison and you came to me.' Then the righteous will answer him, saying, 'Lord, when did we see you hungry and feed you, or thirsty and give you drink? And when did we see you a stranger and welcome you, or naked and clothe you? And when did we see you sick or in prison and visit you?' And the King will answer them, 'Truly, I say to you, as you did it to one of the least of these my brothers, you did it to me.'** (Matt. 25:34-40) and no one in this world will say that the hungry one was the king; it is just an example and a metaphor.

Similarly, Mark said, **"Whoever receives one such child in my name receives me, and whoever receives me, receives not me but Him who sent me."** (Mark 9:37). This passage does not mean that the boy is Jesus (PBUH) himself, or that Jesus (PBUH) is Allah (S.W) Himself. It means that, he (PBUH) tells us that whoever does good deeds for the child, is the same as doing it for him, and is obeying Allah (S.W) and His orders.

Similarly, as anyone who has seen Jesus (PBUH) is considered as if he or she has seen Allah (S.W), then whoever accepts Jesus (PBUH) and his disciples, has accepted Allah (S.W), and whoever has denied their message, he or she – in fact- has denied Allah's Law. Therefore, Jesus (PBUH) said, **"The one who hears you hears me, and the one who rejects you rejects me, and the one who rejects me rejects him who sent me."** (Luke 10:16)

He (PBUH) confirms that again when he said, **"Whoever receives you receives me, and whoever receives me receives him who sent me."** (Matt. 10:40) similarly, whoever has seen Jesus (PBUH) it is the same as seeing Allah (S.W), because, as he said, **"Do you not believe that I am in the Father and the Father is in me? The words that I say to you I do not speak on my own authority, but the Father who dwells in me does his works."** (John 14:10).

In the Book of Acts, when Peter spoke to Ananias regarding the field's money, is similar. **"While it remained unsold, did it not remain your own? And after it was sold, was it not at your disposal? Why is it that you have contrived this deed in your heart? You have not lied to men but to God." When Ananias heard these words, he fell down and breathed his last. And great fear came upon all who heard of it."** (Acts 5:4-5). To lie to people is to lie – in fact - to Allah (S.W), and that does not mean that people and Allah (S.W) are the same.

The seeing, when he said "Who has seen me has seen the Father" is metaphoric, which is the insight seeing and not the sight, and this insight seeing is for all believers, who are from Allah (S.W). Jesus (PBUH) said, **"not that anyone has seen the Father except he who is from God; he has seen the Father."** (John 6:46) and all the believers are from Allah (S.W). **"Everyone who believes that Jesus is the Christ has been born of God, and everyone who**

loves the Father loves whoever has been born of Him." (John (1) 5:1)

Another proof is what Jesus (PBUH) said after that. **"Yet a little while and the world will see me no more, but you will see me. Because I live, you also will live."** (John 14:19) He is not talking about real sight, since he is talking about his ascension to heaven and at that time, the world and the disciples will not see him. He is talking about the faith and spiritual insight, in which the believers and the disciples will be able to see and feel, but not the others.

What comes in Matthew supports this. Matthew said, **"And no one knows the Son except the Father, and no one knows the Father except the Son."** (Matt. 11:27)

Another passage, which is similar, that comes in the Gospel according to John: **"And Jesus cried out and said, "Whoever believes in me, believes not in me but in Him who sent me. And whoever sees me sees Him who sent me. For I have not spoken on my own authority, but the Father who sent me has Himself given me a commandment--what to say and what to speak. And I know that His commandment is eternal life. What I say, therefore, I say as the Father has told me."** (John 12:44-51) and it meant insight.

His saying, "Who has seen me has seen the one who has sent me", does not mean that who has seen the one sent – the Son – has seen the sender – the Father-- unless they both are one. Furthermore, this can be refuted by his saying, **"You heard me say to you, 'I am going away, and I will come to you.' If you loved me, you would have rejoiced, because I am going to the Father, for the Father is greater than I."** (John 14:28) and **"My Father, who has given them to me, is greater than all, and no one is able to snatch them out of the Father's hand."** (John 10:29). No Christian would affirm that the Father is the Son, but they are different personalities, even though they claim that they – the Son and the Father- are united.

In his book, "Commentaries on John's Gospel", Priest Matta El Meskeen said, "Christian belief is that, the hypostases of God are different. The Father is not the Son, nor the Son is the Father, and each hypostasis has his own divine characteristics."[1] Therefore, who has seen the Son, did not see the Father.

Finally, according to the Bible, it is impossible to see Allah (S.W) in this world: **"No one has ever seen God; the only God, who is at the Father's side, he has made him known."** (John 1:18) **"who alone has immortality, who dwells in unapproachable light, whom no one has ever seen or can see. To Him be honor and eternal dominion. Amen.** (Ti. 1 6:16) Therefore, taking this verse "Who has seen me has seen the Father" as evidence for Jesus' divinity is weak and feeble, and is the insight kind of seeing as I mentioned above.

C) Jesus' (PBUH) Everlasting Presence

Those who claim Jesus' (PBUH) divinity cling to some of his words, which speak of his presence with his disciples and their followers, which come in the Gospels. They believe that it is an eternal presence. He said, while he was ascending to heaven, **"teaching them to observe all that I have commanded you. And behold, I am with you always, to the end of the age."** (Matt. 28:20). He said, "Whenever two or three are gathered in my name, I will be among them".

They understand that it is a real physical presence and they consider it as evidence to his divinity, for Jesus (PBUH) is present everywhere and at any time, as Allah (S.W) is everywhere and at any time.[2]

The Holy Bible does not speak of a real physical presence of Allah (S.W) nor of Jesus (PBUH), for Allah (S.W) does not incarnate or dwell in His Creations. His presence is metaphoric; it is a support, and guidance type of presence and the same is for Jesus (PBUH) in showing the right path and instruction.

The passages that contain this kind of presence in the Holy Bible are uncountable. **"You will not need to fight in this battle. Stand firm, hold your position, and see the salvation of the LORD on your behalf, O Judah and Jerusalem.' Do not be them, and the LORD will be with you."** (Chron.2 20:17) **"for the**

---

[1] - The Gospel according to John, Priest Matta El Meskeen, Vol. 1 pp 35
[2] - All these are unacceptable in the Muslim Faith.

LORD your God is He who goes with you to fight for you against your enemies, to give you the victory." (Duet. 20:4)

Allah (S.W) is with them by His salvation and support, and not that He came from heaven and physically fought with them.

Allah's (S.W) presence requires a response from the Jews, which is their acceptance of His Law and worshipping Him. **"and he went out to meet Asa and said to him, "Hear me, Asa, and all Judah and Benjamin: The LORD is with you while you are with Him. If you seek Him, He will be found by you, but if you forsake Him, He will forsake you."** (Chr.2 15:2). And this is proof that it is a metaphoric presence.[1]

Regarding this claimed real presence of Jesus (PBUH), Jesus (PBUH) denied it and refuted this claim, when he told his disciples that he was leaving earth and would not be amongst them. He said, **"For you always have the poor with you, but you will not always have me."** (Matt. 26:11) Jesus then said, **"I will be with you a little longer, and then I am going to Him who sent me."** (John 7:33)

His presence with them was spiritual, as Paul said in his Epistles to the Colossians and the Corinthians. **"Or though I am absent in body, yet I am with you in spirit, rejoicing to see your good order and the firmness of your faith in Christ."** (Col. 2:5) **"For though absent in body, I am present in spirit; and as if present, I have already pronounced judgment on the one who did such a thing."** (Cor.1 5:3)

D) Christ, the Image of Allah (S.W)

Among the evidence Christians present to prove Jesus' (PBUH) divinity, are Paul's words about him. **"the glory of Christ, who is the image of God"** (Cor.2 4:4) **"who, though he was in the form of God, did not count equality with God a thing to be grasped, but made himself nothing, taking the form of a servant, being born in the likeness of men."** (Phi. 2:6-7) **"He is the image of the invisible God, the firstborn of all creation."** (Col. 1:15)

---

[1] - see also, (Gen. 48:21, Exodus 10:10, Chro.(1) 22:18, Jer. 42:11)

These words are Paul's words. Paul, who did not have the honor of meeting Jesus (PBUH) nor did he study under him. We do not see the disciples mention such words, and that is sufficient to throw doubts on them.

Moreover, the image is different from the self. God's image here means His representative to declare His Law, as Paul said in another passage, **"For a man ought not to cover his head, since he is the image and glory of God, but woman is the glory of man."** (Cor. (1) 11/7). Which means that Allah (S.W) delegated man in his power over woman.

Jesus' (PBUH) being of the same image as Allah (S.W) does not prove his divinity, for Adam – according to the Bible – shared Allah's (S.W) image, as mentioned in the Book of Genesis about his creation. **"Then God said, "Let us make man in our image, after our likeness. And let them have dominion over the fish of the sea and over the birds of the heavens and over the livestock and over all the earth and over every creeping thing that creeps on the earth." So God created man in his own image, in the image of God he created him; male and female."**

E. Prostrating to Jesus

The Gospels mention the prostrating of some people, who were contemporary with Jesus (PBUH), to him. Christians believe that this prostrating is evidence of his divinity, and that he is worthy of worship.

The father of the bleeding girl did it once, **"While he was saying these things to them, behold, a ruler came in and knelt before him, saying, "My daughter has just died, but come and lay your hand on her, and she will live."** (Matthew 9/18), the leprous kneeled to him as well, **"And behold, a leper came to him and knelt before him, saying, "Lord, if you will, you can make me clean."** (Matthew 8/2), and the Magi prostrated to him when he was a child. **"And going into the house they saw the child with Mary his mother and they fell down and worshiped him. Then, opening their treasures, they offered him gifts, gold and frankincense and myrrh."** (Matthew 2/11).

There is no doubt that prostrating is an indication of worship, but it does not mean that all prostrating must be worship. Prostrating could be to show esteem and glorification; as Abraham (PBUH) prostrated honoring the people of Hath, **"Abraham rose and bowed to the Hittites, the people of the land."** (Gen. 23/7).

Jacob (PBUH) and his family prostrated to Esau, the son of Isaac, when they met him. (Gen. 33/3-7)

Moses (PBUH) prostrated to his father in law when he came from Median to visit him (Ex. 18:7), and Joseph's brothers (PBUH) prostrated to him not to worship, but to honor him. (Gen. 42:6).

All these examples and many more do not mean more than respect, and the same goes for prostrating to Jesus (PBUH).

4- PASSAGES RELATING ALLAH (S.W)'S CHARACTERISTICS TO JESUS (PBUH)

A. Jesus' Eternity

Christians speak about Jesus (PBUH), the God who existed before creation, and they present their proof in many ways. One of them is to present what comes in the Gospel of John, which the writer attributed to Jesus (PBUH). He said, **"Your father Abraham rejoiced that he would see my day. He saw it and was glad." So the Jews said to him, "You are not yet fifty years old, and have you seen Abraham?" Jesus said to them, "Truly, truly, I say to you, before Abraham was, I am."** (John 8/56-58)

Christians – wrongly – understand from this, that Jesus (PBUH) existed before Abraham (PBUH), which means – according to them – that he is eternal. They support their proof with what John has said about Jesus (PBUH). **"Behold, he is coming with the clouds, and every eye will see him, even those who pierced him, ..."I am the Alpha and the Omega."** (Rev. 1/7-8) (Means the first and the last)

The beginning of the Gospel according to John indicates an eternal existence for Jesus (PBUH) before the creation of the world. **"In the beginning was the Word, and the Word was with God, and the Word was God. He was in the beginning with God.** (John 1/1-2).

These passages – according to Christians- declare the eternity and immortality of Jesus (PBUH); therefore, it is evidence of his divinity.

Scholars do not agree with Christians' conclusions. The existence of Jesus before Abraham (PBUT) does not mean the real existence of him, but the existence of Allah's (S.W) decree and choice of him. That means, that Allah (S.W) had selected him long before He created him, as Paul said, - according to the Monastic Jesuit edition- **"He was foreknown before the foundation of the world"** (Peter (1) 1/20).

Paul said the same about himself and his followers. **"Even as he chose us in him before the foundation of the world, that we should be holy"** (Eph. 1/4) meaning 'Allah (S.W) chose us by his decree as he chose Jesus' (PBUH), and that does not indicate his or their existence at that time.

This old existence of Jesus (PBUH), which is the divine selecting and Allah's (S.W) love of him, is the glory that Allah (S.W) gave to Jesus, as he said, **"And now, Father, glorify me in your own presence with the glory that I had with you before the world existed."** (John 17/5)

This glory is the same glory that Jesus (PBUH) gave to his disciples when he chose them to be his followers, as Allah (S.W) selected him to deliver the message. **"Father, I desire that they also, whom you have given me, may be with me where I am, to see my glory that you have given me because you loved me before the foundation of the world."** (John 17/24). Loving a thing does not need its existence, as one can love the nonexistent or the impossible, which never and will not exist.

Abraham's acquaintance with Jesus (PBUT) before his earthly existence and creation does not mean knowing him personally; for he never saw him. Therefore, his saying, "he saw me and he was delighted", is a figurative and metaphoric seeing, an acquaintance seeing. Otherwise, Christians have to present evidence, proving that Abraham had seen the Son, who is the second hypostasis in the Trinity, or prove the existence of Jesus' body in Abraham's time (PBUT).

Jesus' (PBUH) saying, **"Before Abraham was, I am."** (John 8/56-58) does not prove his existence in the beginning or the eternity. What the passage indicates - if we take it as it is- is that Jesus (PBUH) existed since Abraham's (PBUH) time, but even Abraham's time does not mean eternity.

In addition, if Jesus was before Abraham (PBUT) and all creatures, prophet Jeremiah shared the same existence with him. Allah (S.W) knew Jeremiah and sanctified him before he was born. He said about himself, **"Now the word of the LORD came to me, saying, "Before I formed you in the womb I knew you, and before you were born I consecrated you. I appointed you a prophet to the nations."** (Jeremiah 1 /4-5), and Sirach said in his wisdom, **"who nevertheless was a prophet, sanctified in his mother's womb"** (Sirach 49:7)

This divine acquaintance with Jeremiah, without doubt, is older and more honored than Abraham's acquaintance with Jesus (PBUT), and does not mean his real existence on earth.

Among those who share Jesus' (PBUH) claimed immortality, is Melchizedek, who was a saint in Abraham's time (PBUH). Paul claimed that Melchizedek had neither father nor mother, and no beginning or end, which means he is eternal. Paul said, **"For this Melchizedek, king of Salem, priest of the Most High God, ... He is without father or mother or genealogy, having neither beginning of days nor end of life, but resembling the Son of God he continues a priest forever."** (Heb. 7/1-3)

Why Christians do not consider him as God since he and the Son of God are alike in many ways? He is superior to Jesus (PBUH), whom Christians confess that he was crucified, died, had a mother, and even a father, according to Matthew and Luke, whereas Melchizedek was far above all that.

Furthermore, among those who were before Abraham (PBUH) and deserved eternity- if we do not understand the passages clearly- is human wisdom or, the wise Prophet Solomon (PBUH). He said about himself and about the wisdom, which he and many other humans had, **"I, wisdom, dwell with prudence, and I find knowledge and discretion... "The LORD possessed me at the beginning of his work, the first of his acts of old. I was anointed from everlasting, at the first, before the beginning of the earth. When there were no depths I was brought forth, when there were no springs abounding with water. Before the mountains had been shaped, before the hills, I was brought forth."** (Pro. 8/12-25 Modern King James Version). Thus, Solomon (PBUH), or the wisest of humankind – according to the shallow and literal understanding – is Allah's (S.W) Christ for eternity.

Christians have no evidence for their claim that this passage in Proverbs talks about Jesus (PBUH). Solomon (PBUH) wrote Proverbs, as its introduction says. **"The proverbs of Solomon; son of David."** (Pro. 1/1).

Many passages in Proverbs indicate that Solomon (PBUH) continued to speak these passages when he said, **"My son, be attentive to my wisdom"** (Pro.5/1), and (Proverbs 1/8, 3/1, 3/21, 7/1 and others) the speaker is Solomon (PBUH) and the embodied wisdom in him.

The Holy Bible described Solomon (PBUH) as a wise man, but one may ask which wisdom was it? Was it Allah's (S.W) wisdom, as those, who were contemporary with him, saw in him? **"And all Israel heard of the judgment that the king had rendered, and they stood in awe of the king, because they perceived that the wisdom of God was in him to do justice."** (Kings (1) 3/28).

The sentence, **"I was anointed from everlasting"** (Modern King James Version) does not refer to Jesus (PBUH) the son of Mary (PBUH), as the word 'Messiah', which means anointed, was an attribute for many beside Jesus (PBUH), whom Allah (S.W) had blessed, namely the prophets David and Isaiah (PBUT). (See Psalms 45:7, and Isaiah 1/61).   There is no reason to distinguish Jesus' (PBUH) anointment from the anointment of others.

Facing the interdiction that is caused by the above passage in Proverbs, some Christians say, "the speaker in Proverbs is God's wisdom, which is his personal characteristic that exists in Him from the beginning, and it is not His act which He gave to His prophet Solomon (PBUH). This reasoning is unacceptable, for the passage is talking about a prophet who was anointed with blessing and anointment oil, **"I was anointed from everlasting"**.   Allah's (S.W) characteristic, which exists in Him, can never be anointed, and why should it be?

In addition, the passage is talking about a created wisdom; even though it was old, as the wisdom said, **"The LORD possessed me at the beginning of his work ...Before the mountains had been shaped, before the hills, I was brought forth."**

The Good News Bible (1978-1997), uses the word "Created".   It says, **"The lord created me"** instead of (**The Lord possessed me**).

The Monastic Jesuit Edition uses the same word 'Created'. **"The lord created me first, before his acts"**, thus, the wisdom is an old entity, even before the mountains and the hills.

In Sirach wisdom, **"Wisdom had been created before all things"** (sirach1/4), specifically, **"He created me from the**

beginning before the world, and I shall never fail." (Sirach 24/9). It is not Allah's (S.W) eternal wisdom, but the wisdom He gave to the wise men and incarnated in them. The first one of them was the wise Solomon (PBUH), whom **"they perceived that the wisdom of God was in him."** (Kings (1) 3/28).

Whoever reads the passage thoughtfully, will find no difficulty in understanding which kind of wisdom it was. It is a valuable wisdom; **"for wisdom is better than jewels, and all that you may desire cannot compare with her."** (Pro. 8/11) and it is human; **"The mouth of the righteous brings forth wisdom."** (Pro. 10/31).

The first rank of this human wisdom is Allah (S.W)-fearing; **"The fear of the LORD is the beginning of wisdom"** (Pro. 9/10) and it is Allah's (S.W) gift to man. **"For the LORD gives wisdom; from his mouth come knowledge and understanding"** (Pro. 2/6).

This wisdom is always attached with understanding, the writer advises, **"Say to wisdom, "You are my sister," and call insight your intimate friend, to keep you from the forbidden woman."** (Pro. 7/4-5)

With this wisdom, kings, the rich and the judges, had authority over others. **"I, wisdom, dwell with prudence,.... I have counsel and sound wisdom; I have insight; I have strength. By me kings reign, and rulers decree what is just; by me princes rule, and nobles, all who govern justly. I love those who love me, and those who seek me diligently find me. Riches and honor are with me, enduring wealth and righteousness. My fruit is better than gold, even fine gold, and my yield than choice silver. I walk in the way of righteousness, in the paths of justice, granting an inheritance to those who love me, and filling their treasuries. "The LORD possessed me at the beginning of his work..."** (Pro. 8/ 12-22)

Whoever reads this thoughtfully, will – without doubt - determine that this wisdom is not Allah's (S.W) eternal characteristic, which exists in Him, because there are no jewels or money equal to Allah's (S.W) wisdom, and it brings no wealth, power or dominion. In addition, Allah's (S.W) wisdom does not come from any human mouth, and -

of course - it does not include "Allah (S.W)-fearing", because it is His characteristic.[1]

B.The Beginning of the Gospel According to John

Taking the beginning of the Gospel according to John as evidence for Jesus' (PBUH) divinity, **"In the beginning was the Word, and the Word was with God, and the Word was God. He was in the beginning with God. All things were made through him, and without him was not any thing made that was made."**(John 1/1-3), made scholars point out many important points:

- Scholars brought to our attention, that the writer of this Gospel had plagiarized this passage from Philo Alexandrian (40 C.E.). Phelisian Shali says, "The idea of the Word (logos) comes from the Stoical philosophers and from the Jewish philosopher (Philo), and borrowed from these creeds and theories by Saint Justin, and, by the writer of the first lines of the Gospel, which is attributed to Saint John.[2]

Scholars believe that the term (word) with its philosophical structure is different from Jesus' (PBUH) culture, the simplicity of his words, and the language of his disciples, especially John whom the Book of Acts describes as illiterate and slang-spoken. It says, **"Now when they saw the boldness of Peter and John, and perceived that they were uneducated, common men, they were astonished."** (Acts 4/13)

- Deedat mentioned that there is a fabrication in the English translation, which is the origin of all other translations of the Holy Bible.

---

[1]- The reader may become confused with the description of the wisdom in Proverb: **"then I was beside him, like a master workman, and I was daily his delight, rejoicing before him always, rejoicing in his inhabited world and delighting in the children of man."** (8:30-31) which indicates that the wisdom is a creator. In fact, it is an intended fabrication. The same verse in the Monastic Jesuit Edition, is as follows, **"then I was by him his nursling, and I was daily his delight, rejoicing always before him, rejoicing in his inhabited world"**, it does not talk about the wisdom that creates, but about the child's wisdom, which begins in childhood and grows as the person grows.

[2]- Summary of the History of Religions, Phelsian Challi, pp 247, The Holy Bible's Dictionary, pp 903.

To understand the passage clearly, the prominent scholar Deedat brings us back to the Greek original codex.

The actual translation of that passage is, "in the beginning was the word, and the word was with God". The Greek translation uses the word (hotheos), which translates as "God", in English with the capital 'G' referring to the real divinity.

The passage continues saying, "the word was god", here, the Greek original uses the word (tontheos). The English translation should use the word (god) with a small letter, to indicate the figurative divinity as the Bible uses in many places; I will list a few examples below.

In the Book of Exodus, we read, **"I have made you like God to Pharaoh"** (Exodus 7/1).

When he was talking about the devil that Paul called him the "god of age", who blinded the mind of the unbelievers (see, Cor.2 4:4). The Greek original used the word (tenthoes) in Paul's Epistle, and it translated to (god) in English, using the indefinite article (a).

The Holy Bible English translators changed the Greek passage of John's Gospel, using the word "God" which refers to the real divinity, instead of (god) which refers to the figurative meaning, which makes the confusion in this passage, and that - without doubt – is a kind of fabrication.[1]

Some translations realized this mistranslation and used the correct form of the word; one of them is the New World Translation, in its various universal translations, it says, (and the word was a god).

In addition, I have designated a special appendix to show the distortion in many different copies in reading this word. Some of what I mentioned is, "In John's sentence, whether the Word or Logos was (god) or (divine) or (as god), does not mean that God was with God; it is only a characteristic of the Word or Logos, and it does not determine its identity as God Himself".

I quoted from Phillip Horner, a writer in the Holy Bible Literature Magazine, his saying in (volume 92/87), "I think the description indication in (John 1:1) is so obvious, we cannot consider the name definite"

---

[1] - Two debates in Stockholm, Ahmad Deedat, pp 135-137. Christ in Islam, Ahmad Deedat, pp 84-87

In his Commentary on John's Gospel, the Egyptian priest Matta Al Meskeen said,

"Here the word (God), in the Greek origin, came without the definite article (the)… and since the word (the God) means the whole self. In the second sentence, (the word was god), it is to show the nature of the Word, that it is divine, and does not mean that it is God himself.

Be cautious not to read (God) with the definite article (the) in the sentence, (the word was god). In that case, there will be no difference between the Word and God; consequently, there will be no difference between the Father and the Son. That is the heterodoxy from Sabelius, who said that it is only names, while the Christian belief says: the hypostasis in God is distinctive, the Father is not the Son, nor the Son is the Father, each hypostasis has his special divine function, thus, God is not the Word and the Word is not God."[1]

Even If scholars ignored all that, many things in the passage prevent Christians taking it as evidence of Jesus' divinity:

First: what does the word "beginning", mean? The Christians' answer is "the eternity".

That is not strong evidence, as the word "beginning" comes in the Holy Bible with many other meanings:

-The beginning of creation, as mentioned in **"In the beginning, God created the heavens and the earth"** (Genesis 1/1)

Jesus' (PBUH) description of the devil, that he existed from the beginning, **"You are of your father the devil, and your will is to do your father's desires. He was a murderer from the beginning, and has nothing to do with the truth, because there is no truth in him."** (John 8/44)

What Matthew said quoting Jesus (PBUH), when he was debating the Jews, **"They said to him, "Why then did Moses command one to give a certificate of divorce and to send her away?" He said to them, "Because of your hardness of heart Moses allowed you to divorce your wives, but from the beginning it was not so."** (Matthew 19:7-8) meaning, "That was not permitted when the creation began". The beginning of creation is a created moment and not eternity, which may precede any time.

---

[1]- The Gospel according to John, Father Matta Al Meskeen, Vol.1, pp 35

-The word "Beginning" also means a period, as mentioned in Luke, **"just as those who from the beginning were eyewitnesses and ministers of the word have delivered them to us."** (Luke 1/2), means in the beginning of Jesus' (PBUH) mission.

Likewise, John's saying, **"Beloved, I am writing you no new commandment, but an old commandment that you had from the beginning. The old commandment is the word that you have heard."** (John (1) 2/7)

When Jesus (PBUH) answered the Jews when they asked him, is similar, **"So they said to him, "Who are you?" Jesus said to them, "Just what I have been telling you from the beginning."** (John 8/25)

These uses of the word "beginning" do not mean "eternity", but it means, "Created specific time".

Thus, Christians do not have the right to say that the word "beginning" means "eternity", unless they can prove it undisputedly.

Second: what does the word "Word" mean? Does it mean Jesus (PBUH), or does it have other meanings?

In fact, the Holy Bible mentioned the word "Word" indicating different meanings, some of them are as follows:

- The Holy Bible uses it to indicate God's Books and His inspiration, **"the word of God came to John the son of Zechariah."** (Luke3/2), **"My mother and my brothers are those who hear the word of God and do it."** (Luke 8/21), **"But it is not as though the word of God has failed. For not all who are descended from Israel belong to Israel."** (Rom. 9/6)

- It uses it to indicate the divine orders and authority, which made the creatures. **"By the word of the LORD the heavens were made, and by the breath of his mouth all their host. ... For he spoke, and it came to be; he commanded, and it stood firm."** (Psalms 33/6-9)

That is the reason that Jesus (PBUH) was called a word, because he was created by Allah's (S.W) command, without any human reason (meaning without a father), or because he declared Allah's (S.W) word.

- Allah's (S.W) word can also mean His promise; prophet Jeremiah told about the Israelite people and their urging for the day of curse and punishment, which Allah (S.W) had promised them. **"Behold, they say to me, "Where is the word of the LORD? Let it come!" I have not run away from being your shepherd, nor have I desired the day of sickness."** (Jeremiah 17:15-16)

Jesus (PBUH), according to this, is Allah's (S.W) word, meaning he is the promised word, the good tidings that Allah (S.W) had foretold us by his prophets. (Peace be upon them)

The Christians claimed meaning of the word "Word", which is "Logos", as the second hypostasis of Trinity, does not exist in all the prophet's books.

Third: the sentence "and the word was God", indicates that Jesus (PBUH) was called as God, the same as the judges in the Torah, **"God has taken His place in the divine council; in the midst of the gods He holds judgment. How long will you judge unjustly and show partiality to the wicked?** (Psalms 82:1),

David (PBUH) called the Jewish nobles gods, **"I give you thanks, O LORD, with my whole heart; before the gods I sing your praise"** (Psalms 138:1)

Allah (S.W) told Moses about Aaron (PBUT), **"He shall speak for you to the people, and he shall be your mouth, and you shall be as God to him."** (Exodus. 4:16), and the same for others as stated previously.

Fourth: his saying "the word was with God", the word 'with' here is a preposition; it neither means sameness nor equality. It means Allah (S.W) created the word, as Eve said, **"I have gotten a man from the LORD."** (Gen. 4:1 KJV). Cain is not equal to Allah (S.W) or like Him, even though he came from Allah (S.W). The same meaning came in another passage. **"Then the LORD rained on Sodom and Gomorrah sulfur and fire from the LORD out of heaven.** (Gen. 19:24)

5- THE ATTRIBUTION OF ALLAH'S (S.W) DEEDS TO JESUS (PBUH)

A. The Attribution of Creation to God Almighty by Jesus

Some passages attribute the creation to Allah (S.W) by Jesus (PBUH); Christians take it as evidence of his divinity. Among these passages, Paul's words, **"For by Him all things were created, in heaven and on earth, visible and invisible, whether thrones or dominions or rulers or authorities--all things were created through Him and for Him."** (Col. 1:16 - 17)

In another passage, he said, **"God, who created all things by Jesus Christ."** (Eph. 3:9 KJV)

The same is mentioned in John's Gospel, **"He was in the world, and the world was made through him, yet the world did not know him.** (John 1:10), and the same is in the Epistle to the Hebrews, (Heb. 1:2) and other passages.

First, we notice that the Holy Bible passages attribute the creation only to Allah (S.W). The Book of Genesis says, **"In the beginning, God created the heavens and the earth."** (Gen. 1/1). It did not mention another creator, who shared with Allah (S.W) this creation or was a means by which the creation happened. In the Book of Isaiah, we read, **"Thus says God, the LORD, who created the heavens"** (Isaiah 42:5). In addition, Paul and Barnabas said to the people of Lystra, **"we bring you good news that you should turn from these vain things to a living God, who made the heaven and the earth and the sea and all that is in them."** (Acts 14:15). The Holy Bible never mentions a creator but Allah (S.W).

Paul and John's words are talking about Allah (S.W), who created things by Jesus (PBUH) as He made him perform his miracles(Acts 2/22). It did not mention that Jesus (PBUH) is the creator.

The meaning of all these passages, if we consider them genuine, is that Allah (S.W) has created the creatures and things by Jesus (PBUH). Talking about Trinity hypostasis and its different acts, Priest

James Anis said, "An example of the distinction of their acts is, that the Father created the world by the Son". [1]

This is a strange meaning, which neither the Old Testament's prophets nor Jesus (PBUH) did ever mention. However, Paul's Epistles and John's philosophical Gospel, which derived from the Platonic and the Gnostic philosophies, mention it. The Gnostics believe that God is much honored to create by himself; therefore, He authorized the Word or the angels to act on behalf of Him.

Furthermore, Jesus (PBUH) cannot be the creator of heavens and earth; for he himself is a creature. Even though Christians claim that he is the first creature, he is still a creature, and the creature is different from the Creator. **"He is the image of the invisible God, the firstborn of all creation** (Col. 1/15).

Moreover, he who could not bring himself back to life after he died cannot be the creator of heavens and earth or even to be the means of that creation: **"This Jesus God raised up."** (Acts 2/32). If Allah (S.W) did not raise him, he would not be able to rise from the dead. **"And you killed the Author of life, whom God raised from the dead."** (Acts 3/15), and Paul's words, **"God the Father, who raised him from the dead."** (Galatians 1/1).

Scholars believe that the word creation in these passages means the creation of guidance and leading, and not the real creation from nothing, for that is only Allah's (S.W) work. The creating, which Jesus (PBUH) performed, is the new kind of creating, the guidance creating, which David (PBUH) spoke of when he was praying to Allah (S.W), saying, **"Create in me a clean heart, O God, and renew a right spirit within me."** (Psalms 51:10).

Paul said the same about those who believe in Jesus (PBUH). **"Therefore, if anyone is in Christ, he is a new creation."** (Cor.2, 5/17)

He also said, **"For neither circumcision counts for anything, nor uncircumcision, but a new creation,"** (Galatians 6/15)

On that basis, James considered the disciples as the first creations, he said, **"Of his own will he brought us forth by the word of truth, that we should be a kind of first fruits of his creatures."** (James 1/18), meaning the first guided, who underwent

---

[1]- Methodical Theology, Dr. James Anas, pp 178

a new creation. Thus, Jesus' (PBUH) creating of beings is a spiritual creation; for Allah (S.W) made him awaken the hard-hearted.

One may refute our reasoning and understanding of these passages with what he/she reads in them about the creation of heavens and earth by Jesus (PBUH). He/she may also consider that these passages, which Christians present, do not refer to humans only, but include heaven and earth. This, for those who are not accustomed with the Bible's expression, will prevent the reasoning of this new creation, which I have explained.

Those who are accustomed with the Bible's expression consider these passages as a usual exaggeration of the Old and the New Testaments. Some of these descriptions, I will list below:

The New Testament describes Jesus (PBUH) and the disciples as the light of the world. John said, **"Again Jesus spoke to them, saying, "I am the light of the world. Whoever follows me will not walk in darkness, but will have the light of life."** (John 8/12),

Jesus (PBUH) said to his disciples, **"You are the light of the world."** (Matt. 5:14). As we know, they all were the light, which showed the believers the right path; and was rejected by others whom their hearts were still in darkness.

Christians cannot claim that the light is for animals and the inanimate entities, for, when John describes Jesus (PBUH) and his disciples as the light of the world, they did not light anything except the heart of the believers. He described Jesus (PBUH) as the means of the new creation of the world, meaning the believers only.

Likewise, what Paul said[1] about the conciliation by Jesus' (PBUH) blood, he said, **"and through him to reconcile to himself all things, whether on earth or in heaven, making peace by the blood of his cross."** (Col. 1/20). Even though this conciliation was for the people, not animals or other unbelieving creatures, these have no share in this conciliation, which we may understand from the passages that they were included.

---

[1] - This important passage comes two lines after his words, **"For by him all things were created, in heaven and on earth, visible and invisible, whether thrones or dominions or rulers or authorities--all things were created through him and for him."** (Col. 1:16)

In Ephesus, Paul spoke about those whom Allah (S.W) has sent Jesus (PBUH) to redeem, He sent him in order to, **"as a plan for the fullness of time, to unite all things in him, things in heaven and things on earth"** (Ephesus 1/10).

James Anas said, "the word 'everything' does not mean the universe with its living and inanimate entities, such as the sun, the moon, and the stars, because they cannot be reconciled with God. In addition and for the same reason, it does not mean all the animals and the degraded creatures; for Jesus did not come to ransom the degraded angels (Heb. 2/16), and it does not mean all humans, because the Book knows that not all the people can be reconciled with God."[1]

Likewise, is Paul' saying, **"For as in Adam all die, so also in Christ shall all be made alive."** (Cor.(1) 15/22) If death included all people because of Adam's sin, those whom Jesus brings to life are the believers only, not all the dead that died because of Adam's sin.

Thus, we see in these passages, a general meaning for the word 'Creation' that was not intended for a real creation. It was intended for a special creation that is the guidance creation, which is only for the believers.

B. Judgment's Attribution to Jesus

The Bible speaks of Jesus (PBUH) as the Judge of all creations on the Day of Judgment. Paul said, **"I charge you in the presence of God and of Christ Jesus, who is to judge the living and the dead, and by his appearing and his kingdom."** (2Ti. 4/1) Christians present this passage as evidence of his divinity, because the Torah says, **"for God himself is judge."** (Psalms 50: 6).

However, other passages prove the contrary, and prevent Jesus (PBUH) from being judge, **"For God did not send his Son into the world to judge the world, but in order that the world might be saved through him. He that believeth on him is not judged: he that believeth not hath been judged already, because he hath not believed on the name of the only**

---

[1]- Methodical Theology, Dr. James Anas, pp 724

begotten Son of God." (John 3/17 ASV). Therefore, Jesus will never judge anyone.

John confirmed this again by saying, **"If anyone hears my words and does not keep them, I do not judge him. For, I did not come to judge the world but to save the world. The one who rejects me and does not receive my words has a judge.** Allah (S.W) and his statute) **the word that I have spoken will judge him on the last day."** (John 12:47-48)

Jesus (PBUH), whom Christians claim to be the Judge of all, could not guarantee heaven for his cousins and disciples, sons of Zebedee, because Allah (S.W) did not give him this authority. He, who cannot do so, is incapable of having absolute Judgment. The mother of the two sons came to Jesus (PBUH). After he asked her about her inquiry, she said, **"Say that these two sons of mine are to sit, one at your right hand and one at your left, in your kingdom. Jesus answered,... but to sit at my right hand, and at my left is not mine to grant, but it is for those for whom it has been prepared by my Father."** (Matthew 20/20-22).

If Christians still insist that the judgment is one of Jesus' (PBUH) acts (PBUH), then many others share that with him. Among those are his twelve disciples, including the betrayer Judas. **"Jesus said to them, "Truly, I say to you, in the new world, when the Son of Man will sit on his glorious throne, you who have followed me will also sit on twelve thrones, judging the twelve tribes of Israel."** (Matthew19/28), (see also Luke 22/30)

Paul and the other saints will judge not only the people, but also the angels and the entire world as well. He said, **'Or do you not know that the saints will judge the world?... Do you not know that we are to judge angels?'** (Cor.(1) 6/2-3). They will judge the angels and the whole world but they are not gods, thus, judgment cannot be evidence of divinity, unless we consider all of the above mentioned, gods.

It is worth mentioning here that Jesus' judgment of people -if it is true – is a gift from Allah (S.W) to Jesus the man; he performs it based on his humanity, **"And he has given him authority to execute judgment, because he is the Son of Man."** (John 5/27).

C-   Jesus' Forgiveness of Sins

Among the evidence, which Christians present for Jesus' (PBUH) divinity, is what comes in the Gospels regarding his forgiveness of the paralytic and the sinner woman's sins. Forgiveness, as they believe, is a divine characteristic; thus, Jesus (PBUH) is Allah (S.W) who forgives, as he said to Mary Magdalene, **"Your sins are forgiven."** (Luke 7/48), and he said to the paralytic, **"Take heart, my son; your sins are forgiven."** (Matthew 9/2). The Jews, at that moment, accused him of blasphemy, **"some of the scribes said to themselves, "This man is blaspheming."** (Matthew 9/3) which means: he claims divinity when he forgives the people.

If we read the story of these events, when he forgave these people, we would realize clearly that Jesus (PBUH) was not the one who forgave them. In the sinner woman's story, when people suspected Jesus (PBUH), and after he said to her, **"Your sins are forgiven."** Explaining the confusion, since he is only a human, Jesus (PBUH) told the woman that it is her belief that had redeemed her.

I need to mention here, that Jesus (PBUH) did not claim that he was the one who forgave her. He told her that her sin was forgiven, and the one who forgives, of course, is Allah (S.W).

The story according to Luke is as follows, **"but she has anointed my feet with ointment. Therefore, I tell you, her sins, which are many, are forgiven--for she loved much. But he who is forgiven little, loves little. And he said to her, "Your sins are forgiven. Then those who were at table with him began to say among themselves, "Who is this, who even forgives sins? And he said to the woman, "Your faith has saved you; go in peace."** (Luke 7/46-50), Allah (S.W) forgave her because of her belief, and Jesus (PBUH) told her that she was covered with Allah's (S.W) mercy. He also made it clear to the people, who were present that he did not commit blasphemy and that he did not claim sins' forgiveness.

Likewise, Jesus did not claim that he was the one who forgave the paralytic. He said to him, **"Take heart, my son; your sins are forgiven."** He told him that his sins were forgiven, but he did not mention that he was the one who forgave.

When the Jews thought that Jesus (PBUH) had blasphemed, he scolded them and corrected their evil thoughts. He explained to them that this forgiveness was not from him, but it is Allah's (S.W) authority, and Allah (S.W) permitted him to do so, as He permitted him to perform all his miracles. They understood what he meant, and their misunderstanding disappeared. **"When the crowds saw it, they were afraid, and they glorified God, who had given such authority to men."** (Matthew 9/8)

This authority is not Jesus' (PBUH) characteristic; it is Allah's (S.W) permission, who gave it to him. If Jesus (PBUH) is God, that would be his own characteristic and his own authority, but he cannot perform anything except what Allah (S.W) permitted him to do. He is a servant of Allah (S.W), as he said, **"All things have been handed over to me by my Father."** (Luke 10/22), he has no power without Allah (S.W). He said in another place, **"All authority in heaven and on earth has been given to me"** (Matthew 28/18).

He said about his capability, **"I can do nothing on my own."** (John 5/30). If it was not with Allah's (S.W) help, he would not be able to forgive a sin.

The Jews asked Jesus (PBUH), **"Tell us by what authority you do these things, or who it is that gave you this authority?"** (Luke 20/2-4). Jesus (PBUH) did not claim that it was his own authority, which he gained from his eternal divinity, instead, he asked them about John the Baptist's (PBUH) authority of forgiveness, where was it from. He said, **"I also will ask you a question. Now tell me Was the baptism of John from heaven or from man?"** (Luke 20/2-4). This means that all he did, forgiveness and other things, were by the same authority as that of John the Baptist (PBUH); and it was no more than the prophet-hood authority.

Forgiveness was not only for Jesus (PBUH), it was the authority of his disciples, but they were not gods, although, they were able to forgive sins, not only related to their own rights, but also all sins. Regarding forgiveness related to their own rights, Jesus said, **"For if you forgive others their trespasses, your heavenly Father will also forgive you. But if you do not forgive others their trespasses, neither will your Father forgive your trespasses."** (Matthew 6/14-15).

John gave the disciples open authority to forgive any sin, he said, **"If you forgive the sins of anyone, they are forgiven; if you withhold forgiveness from anyone, it is withheld."** (John

20/23). Hence, they were like Jesus (PBUH), but no one considers them gods.

The church gave itself the claimed authority of Peter and the disciples. Priests were able to forgive sinners by confession or by the indulgence, claiming that they had inherited this authority from Peter. **"I will give you the keys of the kingdom of heaven, and whatever you bind on earth shall be bound in heaven, and whatever you loose on earth shall be lost in heaven."** (Matthew 16/19). Therefore, if Peter or the Pope – his successor- forgave one's sin, he or she will be forgiven, and that will not make Peter or the Pope god.

This authority was not only for Peter and his successors, but also for all the disciples. **"Truly, I say to you, whatever you bind on earth shall be bound in heaven, and whatever you loose on earth shall be loosed in heaven. Again I say to you, if two of you agree on earth about anything they ask, it will be done for them by my Father in heaven."** (Matthew 18/18-20). That – obviously- does not mean that they are gods, because it is not a personal right for them, but a gift from Allah (S.W) to them and to their master, Jesus (PBUH), this is what the Holy Bible says.

6- JESUS' MIRACLES AS EVIDENCE OF HIS DIVINITY

The Gospels mention thirty-five miracles, which Jesus (PBUH) performed, and Christians take these miracles as proof of his divinity. These miracles are, his birth without a father, giving life to the dead, curing the sick and telling the unseen.

Miracles are Divine Gifts

The Quran mentions and confirms Jesus' (PBUH) great miracles, and affirms that he did these miracles by the will and the help of Allah (S.W). **"And (appoint him) an apostle to the Children of Israel. (with this message), "'I have come to you, with a Sign from your Lord, in that I make for you out of clay, as it were, the figure of a bird, and breathe into it, and it becomes a bird by God's leave, And I heal those born blind, and the lepers, and I quicken the dead, by God's leave; and I declare to you what ye eat, and what ye store in your houses."** (Holy Quran 3: 49)

The Gospels' passages confirmed this, and reported about Jesus (PBUH), as when he performed his miracles he declared that they were from Allah (S.W), he did not attribute them to himself. Jesus (PBUH) said, **"It is by the Spirit of God that I cast out demons."** (Matthew 12/28)

He also said, **"It is by the finger of God that I cast out demons."** (Luke 11/ 20).

When he (PBUH) came to give life to Lazarus, **"And Jesus lifted up his eyes and said, "Father, I thank you that you have heard me I knew that you always hear me, but I said this on account of the people standing around, that they may believe that you sent me."** (John 11/40-41). He thanked Allah (S.W) for His acceptance of his prayer, and supplication when he raised his eyes to Allah (S.W), then God responded to him and gave life to Lazarus.

He also prayed to Allah (S.W) to help him when he wanted to feed the crowd with the five loaves and two fish. **"And taking the five**

loaves and the two fish, he looked up to heaven and said a blessing. Then he broke the loaves." (Matthew 14/19).

When he cured the deaf, he prayed to Allah (S.W) as well, "**And looking up to heaven, he sighed and said to him, "Ephphatha," that is, "Be opened". And his ears were opened, his tongue was released, and he spoke plainly.**" (Mark 7/34-35). Allah (S.W) did not disappoint him in his supplication, praying and asking for help.

Talking about his miracles and wonders, Jesus (PBUH) said, "**All authority in heaven and on earth has been given to me.**" (Means from Allah (S.W)) (Matthew 28/ 18). All what he had were gifts from Allah (S.W). If he was God, his miracles would come from his divine nature, and need no one to help or give them to him.

In addition, the same authority was given to the devil without being God, he said to Jesus (PBUH), trying to mislead him of the earth's property. "**To you I will give all this authority and their glory, for it has been delivered to me, and I give it to whom I will.**" (Luke 4/6).

Jesus (PBUH) declared also that he was helpless without Allah's (S.W) help and aid. He said, "**I can do nothing on my own.**" (John 5/30), and these miracles were Allah's (S.W) gifts, which prove his prophethood only. "**For the works that the Father has given me to accomplish, the very works that I am doing bear witness about me that the Father has sent me.**" (John 5/36).

Furthermore, those who witnessed Jesus' (PBUH) miracles knew that what he was performing were miracles, which Allah (S.W) gave to his messengers. No one understood that those miracles were evidence of his divinity. When the boy recovered from the unclean spirit, everyone was astonished by the greatness of Allah (S.W). "**And all were astonished at the majesty of God.**" (Luke 9/43)

Moreover, when he cured the hunchback woman, she stood straight and praised Allah (S.W). "**And immediately she was made straight, and she glorified God.**" (Luke 13/13)

When the crowd saw Jesus (PBUH) curing the paralytic, they were astonished, and praised Allah (S.W) who gave man such power.

"They were afraid, and they glorified God, who had given such authority to men." (Matthew 9:8)
They considered Jesus (PBUH) as one of the people, a man, and not God, and his ability to cure was from Allah (S.W), the Healer.

The blind man, whom Jesus (PBUH) healed, according to the Gospel of John, considered Jesus (PBUH) as a man only. **"So they said to him, "Then how were your eyes opened? He answered, "The man called Jesus".**" (John 9/10-11) Do those people, who conclude Jesus' (PBUH) divinity for curing the blind man, know, love and care for Jesus more than that blind man?

When Jesus (PBUH) rebuked the wind and the sea and they obeyed him, the witnesses did not understand that he was divine, in spite of the greatness of this miracle, but instead they wondered about the power of Jesus the man. Matthew said, **"And the men marveled, saying, "What sort of man is this, that even winds and sea obey him?"** (Matthew 8/27).

At the time when Martha, Lazarus' sister, asked Jesus (PBUH) to give life to her brother, she assured him of her knowledge that these miracles were from Allah (S.W), who gave it to Jesus (PBUH) to aid and support him.   She said, **"But even now I know that whatever you ask from God, God will give you."** (John 11/22).

Confirming the same idea, Peter, the leader of the disciples said to the crowd, **"Jesus of Nazareth, a man attested to you by God with mighty works and wonders and signs that God did through him."** (Acts 2/22).

Nicodemus, the teacher of The Law, realized the secret of Jesus' (PBUH) great miracles, and that they were from Allah (S.W) and because of His help and aid to Jesus (PBUH). He said to Jesus (PBUH), **"Rabbi, we know that you are a teacher come from God, for no one can do these signs that you do unless God is with him."** (John 3/2).

The Gospels also declare that these miracles are no more than gifts from Allah (S.W), and Jesus (PBUH) was cautious that he could not do it all the time. Therefore, when he came to the dead man Lazarus, he was worried that he might not be able to do a miracle. **"Some of them said, "He gives sight to the blind. Why couldn't he** have kept Lazarus from dying? Jesus was still terribly upset.” (John 11/37-38. Contemporary English Version)

At other times, the Pharisees asked him for signs, and he (PBUH) could not or did not do them. **“The Pharisees came out and started an argument with Jesus. They wanted to test him by asking for a sign from heaven. Jesus groaned and said, "Why are you always looking for a sign? I can promise you that you will not be given one!”** (Mark 8/11-12).

When the crowd of the Jews gathered asking him (PBUH) for a sign, he did not respond. Instead, he said, **“Jesus replied: You want a sign because you are evil and won't believe! But the only sign you will get is the sign of the prophet Jonah”** (Matthew. 12/38-39).

Moreover, if what Jesus (PBUH) was doing and performing were evidence of his divinity, why did he ask people to hide it, even though it was the way, which people will know his identity? Jesus (PBUH) said to the leprous that he healed, **“Don't tell anyone about this.”** (Mark 1/44),

Regarding the healing of the two blind people, Matthew said, **“and Jesus strictly warned them not to tell anyone about him.”** (Matthew 9/31 International Standard Version) Jesus (PBUH) also said to a third blind man, when he healed him, **"Don't go into the village or tell anyone in the village.”** (Mark 8/26).

He (PBUH) said that frequently: **“Jesus, aware of this, withdrew from there. And many followed him, and he healed them all. and ordered them not to make him known.”** (Matthew 12/15-16). By hiding his miracles, Jesus (PBUH) did not want the people to be occupied by his miracles and forget his real mission. If it was evidence of his divinity , he should have told them.

Miracles Do Not Indicate - According to the Bible – Prophethood, Never Mind Divinity

I wonder that Christians consider Jesus' (PBUH) miracles as evidence of his divinity, since the Holy Bible declares that other people had performed such great miracles, without considering that as evidence of their divinity.

The Holy Bible confirms these miracles and many more magnificent miracles, to all those who believe in Jesus. Jesus (PBUH) said, **"Truly, truly, I say to you, whoever believes in me will also do the works that I do; and greater works than these will he do."** (John 14/12). This means that those who believe in Allah (S.W) can heal the sick, give life to the dead, and can do greater than that; thus, it is not evidence of divinity.

Performing miracles- according to the Bible- cannot be evidence for a true belief or of the honesty of its performer. Then, how can it be proof of prophethood or divinity? Jesus (PBUH) mentioned that liars could perform miracles and claim doing it by his name.

Quoting Jesus (PBUH), Matthew said, **"Not everyone who says to me, 'Lord, Lord,' will enter the kingdom of heaven, but the one who does the will of my Father who is in heaven. On that day many will say to me, 'Lord, Lord, did we not prophesy in your name, and cast out demons in your name, and do many mighty works in your name? And then will I declare to them, 'I never knew you; depart from me, you workers of lawlessness."** (Matthew 7/21-23)

Those hypocrites and liars could do miracles, but it did not prove their honesty, nor will it prove their prophethood or divinity.

Further more, according to the Holy Bible, even a sinner can perform many miracles and wonders, and that does not prove his honesty or divinity, for he or she performs these miracles and wonders, by the aid of Satan and his power. Paul said, **"The coming of the lawless one is by the activity of Satan with all power and false signs and wonders."** (Thessalonians (2) 2/9).

Others Who Shared Jesus' Power of Performing Miracles

Scholars have noticed - after reading the Bible - that messengers and others had shared Jesus' (PBUH) power in performing his miracles, and Christians do not consider these people divine. That indicates that these miracles are proof and evidence that they are prophets, otherwise, Christians have to attribute divinity to all those who performed the same miracles as Jesus (PBUH), which Allah (S.W) made possible for Jesus (PBUH).

A. The Virgin Birth

Jesus' (PBUH) birth, without a father, was one of his greatest miracles. Those who believe in his divinity use it as their evidence. Yaseen Mansour said, "If Jesus was not born of a virgin, he would be just a man".[1]

It is a fact that Jesus (PBUH) was just a man; the proof is that some creatures shared with him this great miracle. The origin of all creatures, including humans, was without father or mother. The creation of Adam (PBUH), who was a complete and perfect creature, is bigger and greater than the creation of Jesus (PBUH), who was a fetus in his mother's womb, born, and then grew up.

No doubt, that being born without a father is a miracle, but it does not conclude or indicate one's divinity. If so, it must have concluded the divinity of many animals and the divinity of Adam and Eve, for Adam was born without a father or mother, and Eve came from Adam without a mother.

Regarding that, Allah (S.W) tells us in the Holy Quran, saying, **"The similitude of Jesus before God is as that of Adam; He created him from dust, then said to him: "Be". And he was."** (Holy Quran 3:59).

In spite of the likeness between Jesus and Adam (PBUT) in their birth, Adam ranks higher than Jesus does in many ways. Adam (PBUH) did not come from a woman's womb covered with blood; God commanded the angels to kneel to him, God taught him all the names, and heaven was his home. In addition, Allah (S.W) spoke to him by Himself without a messenger, and many other things, which neither Jesus (PBUH) nor the others had. Thus, since Adam has all these characteristics, why do Christians not consider him divine?

The same goes for angels, for Allah (S.W) created them without father or mother. They are not made of mud, but Christians do not consider them Gods. Therefore, the virgin birth cannot be evidence of divinity, even though it is a unique event in man's history.

---

[1]- Christianity without Christ, Kamel Sasfan, pp 62. The True Christianity that Jesus taught, Alaa Abu Bakar, pp 186

B. Giving Life to the Dead

No doubt, giving life to the dead was one great miracle among the many that Jesus (PBUH) performed, which the Quran confirms and tells that it was from Allah (S.W). **"and I quicken the dead, by God's leave."** (Holy Quran 3:49).

However, Christians refuse to relate Jesus' power to Allah's (S.W) will, and believe that he was doing that by himself and by his own will. One of their reasons is that he (PBUH) said, **"For as the Father raises the dead and gives them life, so also the Son gives life to whom he will For as the Father has life in himself, so he has granted the Son also to have life in himself."** (John 5/21-26).

If we read the passage carefully, we will see that it talks about the gifts that Allah (S.W) gave to Jesus (PBUH), **"He has granted the Son"**, which he has no power to do or to have without Allah (S.W) giving them to him.

If Christians continue reading the passage, they will find an obvious answer from Jesus (PBUH) to their claim. He said, **"I can do nothing on my own."** (John 5/30).

He (PBUH) continued and explained to them that his will, when he gives life to the dead, is dependant on Allah's (S.W) will. **"Because, I seek not my own will but the will of Him who sent me"** (John 5/30).

Christians insist that giving life to the dead is evidence of Jesus' (PBUH) divinity, and ignore many passages, which attribute that deed to others. Why do Christians not consider them gods?

Indeed, Christian avoidance in considering the divinity of those is evidence of their false claim. If Jesus gave life to Lazarus, (John 11/41-44), the prophet Elijah gave life to the son of the widow. In the First Book of Kings we read, **"And he cried to the LORD, "O LORD my God, have you brought calamity even upon the widow with whom I sojourn, by killing her son? Then he stretched himself upon the child three times and cried to the LORD, "O LORD my God, let this child's life come into him again. And the LORD listened to the voice of Elijah. And the life of the child came into him again, and he**

revived." (Kings (1) 17/20-22) Therefore, Joshua the son of sirach told him, **"Who didst raise up a dead man from death"** (sirach 48\5).

Elijah (PBUH) - with Allah's (S.W) will - also raised two dead people. He raised one of them during his life and the other after his death. He gave life to the Israelite woman's son, who came to him. (Kings (2) 4/32-36)

Not only did Elijah (PBUH) raise a dead man while he was alive, but also his bones, after his death, gave life to another dead man. The relatives of that dead man put him inside Elijah's grave. He returned to life after touching Elijah's bones, and he stood up. **"And as a man was being buried, behold, a marauding band was seen and the man was thrown into the grave of Elisha, and as soon as the man touched the bones of Elisha, he revived and stood on his feet."** (Kings (2) 13/21)

I wonder how Christians could use Jesus' (PBUH) miracles – especially raising the dead - as proof of his divinity, even though they believed that the disciples had done the same.

In the Book of Acts, we read that Peter gave life to Tabitha after she had died and was washed by her family. **"Now there was in Joppa a disciple named Tabitha, which, translated, means Dorcas. In those days she became ill and died, and when they had washed her, they laid her in an upper room. But Peter put them all outside, and knelt down and prayed; and turning to the body he said, "Tabitha, arise." And she opened her eyes, and when she saw Peter she sat up."**(Acts 9/36-41)

I wonder, what is the difference between Jesus' (PBUH) and Peter's miracles? Both miracles were by Allah's (S.W) will and aid.

According to the Holy Bible, all disciples were capable of giving life to the dead. Jesus (PBUH) said, **"And proclaims as you go, saying, 'The kingdom of heaven is at hand. Heal the sick, raise the dead, and cleanse lepers, cast out demons."** (Matthew 10/7-8) so, are all of them gods?

Christians who speak of Jesus' (PBUH) divinity ignore the passages that speak of his death, and his being unable to escape it. He was unable to get his life back until Allah (S.W) gave it to him and raised him from the dead.

Thus, this wonderful miracle, which is giving life to the dead, cannot be used as evidence of Jesus'(PBUH) divinity, but it is a great miracle that Allah (S.W) gave Jesus (PBUH) the ability to perform them as proof of the prophethood of this great prophet, peace be upon him.

C. Healing the Sick

Christians conclude their belief in Jesus' (PBUH) divinity by his miracle of healing the sick. If Jesus (PBUH) had healed the leprous, (Matthew 8/3) Elijah had also healed a leper. In addition, he caused another and his descendants to be leprous. **"And Elisha sent a messenger to him, saying, "Go and wash in the Jordan seven times, and your flesh shall be restored, and you shall be clean. The leprosy of Naaman shall cling to you and to your descendants forever. So he went out from his presence a leper, like snow."** (Kings (2) 5/10-27)

D. Telling the Unseen

Jesus (PBUH) predicted many invisible and unseen matters, and it came as he said. He told the two disciples whom he sent to slaughter the sacrifice at Easter, of what would happen. (Mark 14/12-16)

In addition, Peter said to Jesus (PBUH), **"Lord, you know everything."** (John 21/17). Jesus also knew that no one had ridden the foal, which was tied in 'Bet Fajy' village. This according to priest Ibrahim Saed is solid proof. He said, "It is new evidence of Jesus knowing the unseen in details, with no doubt or interpretation, and that also is evidence of the humble glory that Jesus had".[1]

Jesus (PBUH) was not the only one who predicted the unseen. Jacob (PBUH) predicted the unseen before Jesus (PBUH), as he said to his children, **"Gather yourselves together, that I may tell you what shall happen to you in days to come."** (Gen. 49/1-27)

---

[1]- Commentary on the Gospel according to Luke, pp 475

The same happened with Samuel and Elijah (Samuel (1) 10/2-9), Kings (1) 21/21-24), and their prediction came true, as we read in the Second Book of Kings. (Kings (2) 10/1-17, 9/30-37) Many other similar passages are in the sacred books. (Samuel (1) 19/23-24, Kings (2) 4/8-18, 8/12-13, John 11/49-52)

E. Controlling Devils

Jesus (PBUH) had control or power over devils. (Matthew 12/27-28), but it was also a miracle that was performed by others.

When the Jews accused him of casting out devils by the aid of the devils' leader, he said, **"And if I cast out demons by Beelzebul, by whom do your sons cast them out?"** (Matt. 12:27). As such, he proved that the Jews have the same ability of controlling devils.

Jesus (PBUH) warned us of liars who would succeed in casting out devils. He said, **"On that day many will say to me, 'Lord, Lord, did we not prophesy in your name, and cast out demons in your name, and do many mighty work in your name?"** (Matthew 7/22-23). False prophets are able to bring out devils, but that does not prove their prophethood, their righteousness, or their divinity.

F. Other Miracles

The Gospels mention many other miracles of Jesus (PBUH); turning the water into wine (John 2/7-9); feeding a large crowd with five loves and two fish (Matthew 14/19-21); and the drying up of the fig tree by his words. (Matthew 21/18-19) Christians also mention the great darkness that happened on the day of his claimed death on the cross. (Matthew 27/45). All of these wonders – according to Christians -prove his divinity and that he is the son of Allah (S.W).

In addition, Christians conclude his divinity (PBUH) from the wind and the sea's obedience to him, and that he had power over nature. **"There arose a great storm on the sea, so that the boat was being swamped by the waves; but he was asleep. And they went and woke him, saying, "Save us, Lord; we are perishing. And he said to them, "Why are you afraid, O you of little faith?" Then he rose and rebuked the winds and the sea, and there was a great calm. And the men marveled,**

saying, "What sort of man is this, that even winds and sea obey him?" (Matthew 8:24-27)

Who is the controller of the winds and the sea? Christians find no answer, according to their simple understanding, except saying, he is Jesus (PBUH). He also fasted for forty days without feeling hunger. That is supernatural and no man can do that, and thus, – according to Christians - is proof that Jesus is Allah (S.W). (Matthew 4:1-2)

Others performed the same miracles and no Christian would claim their divinity. If Jesus (PBUH) turned the water into wine, (see John 2:7-9), Moses (PBUH) could turn the water into blood. **"You shall take some water from the Nile and pour it on the dry ground, and the water that you shall take from the Nile will become blood on the dry ground."** (Exodus. 4:9)

Elijah performed greater miracle than that. He filled the empty vessels with oil. **"Go outside, borrow vessels from all your neighbors, empty vessels and not too few. Then go in and shut the door behind yourself and your sons and pour into all these vessels. And when one is full, set it aside. So she went from him and shut the door behind herself and her sons. And as she poured they brought the vessels to her. When the vessels were full, she said to her son, "Bring me another vessel." And he said to her, "There is not another." Then the oil stopped flowing. She came and told the man of God, and he said, "Go, sell the oil and pay your debts, and you and your sons can live on the rest."** (Kings (2) 4:3-7)

If Jesus (PBUH) fed five hundred people with five loaves and two fish, (See, Matt. 14:19-21) Moses (PBUH) fed the Children of Israel, who numbered about six hundred thousand people, Manna and honey for forty years, and all that was by the blessings of Allah (SW). (See Ex. 16:35-36)

In addition, if Jesus (PBUH) turned the fig tree into a dry one, (Matthew 21/18-19), Moses (PBUH) turned a stick into a snake, (Ex. 7/9), which is greater. We can relate the drying of the tree to the laws of nature, but turning a stick into a snake is a miracle in every way.

Regarding the darkness, which Christians claim occurred at Jesus' (PBUH) crucifixion; it is not – in any way – greater than the darkness, which lasted for three days in Egypt when the Egyptians did not believe Moses (PBUH). **"So Moses stretched out his hand toward heaven, and there was pitch darkness in all the land of Egypt three days. They did not see one another, nor did anyone rise from his place for three days."** (Ex. 10:22-23)

Similarly, is what happened when Joshua fought the Amorites, and it was Saturday night; he prayed to Allah (S.W) and said, **"in the sight of Israel, "Sun, stand still at Gibeon, and moon, in the Valley of Aijalon. And the sun stood still, and the moon stopped, until the nation took vengeance on their enemies. The sun stopped in the midst of heaven and did not hurry to set for about a whole day."** (Joshua 10:12-13). What happened on that day does not indicate Joshua's divinity, even though it is greater than what happened during the crucifixion. If the sun had set for three hours, it could be hidden by clouds, and that is normal, but for the earth to stop rotating, is much more significant.

Prophet Isaiah performed greater miracles than both of them did; Allah (S.W) turned the sun backwards for him answering his prayer, to prove to King Hezekiah the truth and the accuracy of Allah's (S.W) decrees. (See, Kings (2) 20/10-11). This is confirmed by Sirach; **"In his time the sun went backward."** (Sirach 48/23). In spite of this, no one claims Isaiah's divinity.

If nature obeyed Jesus (PBUH), many other prophets were able to control it as well, as the fire and the sea obeyed Elijah. The Bible says, **"If I am a man of God, let fire come down from heaven and consume you and your fifty." Then fire came down from heaven and consumed him and his fifty."** (Kings (2) 1:10) **"Then Elijah took his cloak and rolled it up and struck the water, and the water was parted to the one side and to the other, till the two of them could go over on dry ground."** (Kings (2) 2:8),

Jesus (PBUH) fasting for forty days does not prove his divinity, for he felt hungry eventually. **"He was hungry"** (Matthew 4:2) If his fasting and his patience indicate his divinity, then his hunger refutes that and proves his humanity.

I have to remind the reader that Moses and Elijah (PBUT) also fasted for forty days and forty nights. Moses (PBUH) said, **"I remained on the mountain forty days and forty nights. I neither ate bread nor drank water."** (Duet. 9:9), **"went in the strength of** that food forty days and forty nights to Horeb, the mount of God." (Kings1 19:7-8)

<u>VERSES THAT CONTRADICT JESUS'(PBUH) DIVINITY</u>

Scholars have agreed that human deeds, which Jesus (PBUH) performed all his life, prevent and refute calling him Allah (S.W) or the Son of Allah (S.W). It is impossible and incorrect to believe that Allah (S.W) was born, ate, circumcised, beaten, then died.

It is unacceptable reasoning from Christians to say that these deeds were done by the human part of him and not the divine, for they do not believe that Allah's (S.W) incarnation in Jesus (PBUH) was like a dress, which he can put on some times and take off at other times.

What he (PBUH) did must be from the incarnated God, as they claim. Otherwise, they have to agree that he is human, which is fact.

In his letter to Theodosius Caesar, Saint Kerliss, the Bishop of Alexandria, said, "We do not split the human part of Jesus from the divine, nor do we split the word from the human part after that unknown unity, which we cannot explain. We confess that Jesus is from two wills that united and became one, not by destroying the two natures or by their mixture, but by an amazing and noble unity."

Pope Euthenasius said, "This one God is the Son of God spiritually, and he is the Son of man bodily, but that does not mean that the only Son has two natures, one divine and one human, but one nature of the incarnated God's Word, to whom we prostrate, the same as we prostrate to Jesus."

Translating the sentence 'this is my beloved son', Saint Gregarious said, "If I see that my son is hungry, thirsty, sleepy or tired...do not think it is for his body without his divinity. If you see him cure the ills, clean the lepers and make eyes of mud, do not think that he is doing so by his divine part without the human part, because it is not that the great deeds are for one and the humble ones for another."[1]

We will be able to understand this – claimed- unity relationship, which is the unity of the human and the divine parts of Jesus (PBUH), when we realize two different deeds that Jesus performed,

---

[1] - The Frank opinion about the will and nature of Christ, Pastor Gebrial abdel Maseeh, pp 59-60

one through his human part and the other through his divine part. In the story of the bleeding woman, we read, **"She came up behind him and touched the fringe of his garment, and immediately her discharge of blood ceased. And Jesus said, "Who was it that touched me?" When all denied it, Peter said, "Master, the crowds surround you and are pressing in on you! But Jesus said, "Someone touched me, for I perceive that power has gone out from me."** (Luke 8:44-46). In the blink of an eye, Christians compile total divinity with total humanity; Jesus did not know who touched him by his human part, and he cured her by his divine part and all in one moment.

In order to refute this strange unity, all one has to do is to imagine mixing two different elements completely and the properties of each remain the same; if we mix sweet with sour, supposedly – according to Christian understanding- the mixture could be sweet-sour at the same time.

Tens of the Gospels' passages speak of Jesus' (PBUH) human weaknesses, driving him away from divine rank, and answer and refute those who claim his divinity. These passages fall under four categories:

First Category

These are verses and passages, which declare his incapability and weaknesses. Therefore, he cannot be completely human and completely divine at the same time as Christians claim, but only human.

Jesus (PBUH) did not know many things. One of them, which is too important, was that he did not know the time of the Day of Judgment. He said, **"But concerning that day or that hour, no one knows, not even the angels in heaven, nor the Son, but only the Father."** (Mark 13:32). How can Christians claim that he is Allah (S.W) since the nescience of the unknown disputes it?

Not only that Jesus (PBUH) did not know the time of the Day of Judgment, but also he did not know anything except what Allah (S.W) showed him. That is why, when he wanted to raise Lazarus again, **"he was deeply moved in his spirit and greatly troubled. And he said, "Where have you laid him?"** (John 11:33-34)

When a man came to Jesus (PBUH) and asked him to cure his insane son, Jesus (PBUH) did not know how long that son had been sick. **"And Jesus asked his father, "How long has this been happening to him?" And he said, "From childhood."** (Mark 9:21)

Jesus (PBUH) also showed, while he was performing his miracles, that he could not do them without the will and the help of Allah (S.W). He said, **"I can do nothing on my own. As I hear, I judge, and my judgment is just, because I seek not my own will but the will of him who sent me."** (John 5:30)

He (PBUH) affirmed this meaning when he said, **"I can do nothing on my own. As I hear, I judge, and my judgment is just, because I seek not my own will but the will of him who sent me. And he who sent me is with me. He has not left me alone, for I always do the things that are pleasing to him."** (John 8:28-29). In another passage, he said to the Jews, **"Truly, truly, I say to you, the Son can do nothing of his own accord, but only what he sees the Father doing. For whatever the Father does, that the Son does likewise."** (John 5:19)

In addition, Jesus (PBUH) had no authority for good or bad even for himself, except by the mercy and the will of Allah (S.W). When the mother of Zabadee's children, who were his disciples, came to him, **"he said to her, "What do you want?" She said to him, "Say that these two sons of mine are to sit, one at your right hand and one at your left, in your kingdom." Jesus answered, but to sit at my right hand and at my left is not mine to grant, but it is for those for whom it has been prepared by my Father."** (Matt.20:20-22)

The Holy Bible also, in many passages, describes Jesus (PBUH) as a servant of Allah (S.W). In Matthew we read, **"My servant whom I have chosen."** (Matt. 12:18) and in Acts, **"glorified his servant Jesus, the Holy and Righteous One."** (Acts 3:13-14); **"God, having raised up his servant, sent him to you first"** (Acts 3:26), **"your holy servant Jesus."** (Acts 4:30)

Some translations, like the famous Vandyke translation, changed the word 'servant' to the word 'Child', which indicates son-ship. The Jesuit Fathers' translation and the majority of other translations still use the word 'Servant'.

To explain this misguiding change clearly, we read Matthew's words. He said, **"This was to fulfill what was spoken by the prophet Isaiah: "Behold My Child whom I have chosen; My Beloved, in whom My soul is well pleased. I will put My Spirit on Him, and He shall declare judgment to the nations."**(Matt. 12:17-18) Matthew used the word 'Child', but in Isaiah, from which Matthew quoted, the word is 'servant'. **"Behold my servant, whom I uphold, my chosen, in whom my soul delights; I have put my Spirit upon him; he will bring forth justice to the nations."** (Isaiah 42:1)

Second Category

These are verses and passages, which declare his human deeds (PBUH), which are the same as any human being.

Scholars studied the life of Jesus (PBUH) - as mentioned in the Gospels- and they found that he is not different from the rest of human beings. They studied it from the time of the angel's good news to his mother, his birth, his usage of nappies, his circumcision, his growth and education with children, his baptism by John the Baptist, until his assumed death, after his grief praying to Allah (S.W) to save him. Like the rest of us, he was born, he grew, he ate, he slept and died, so what is the thing that makes him different from us and makes him divine?

Covered with blood, he came out of a woman's womb. **"And while they were there, the time came for her to give birth."** (Luke 2:6)

He was breastfed, **"As he said these things, a woman in the crowd raised her voice and said to him, "Blessed is the womb that bore you, and the breasts at which you nursed!"** (Luke 11:27). One may ask the following question, did Mary know that her child, who came out of her womb and whom she took care of as any child, is Allah (S.W), as Christians claim, or did she not?

They circumcised him (PBUH) when he was eight days old. **"And at the end of eight days, when he was circumcised, he was called Jesus"** (Luke 2:21). Did the person who circumcised him know that he was circumcising a God, and what happened to that piece of flesh when split from the incarnated Gods' body? Did it become un-divine or did it remain divine and lost or buried?

John the Baptist baptized Jesus (PBUT) in the River Jordan. **"Then Jesus came from Galilee to the Jordan to John, to be baptized by him"** (Matt. 3:13). Did the Baptist not know that he was baptizing Allah (S.W)? Baptism is for repentance and the cleaning of sins, as mentioned in Matthew. **"And they were baptized by him in the river Jordan, confessing their sins. I baptize you with water for repentance. Then Jesus came from Galilee to the Jordan to John, to be baptized by him."** (Matt. 3:6-13). Was Allah (S.W) a sinner looking for someone to forgive him?

Furthermore, Jesus (PBUH) did what any human needs to do. He slept, **"he was asleep"** (Matt. 8:24) he felt tired as every human does, **"so Jesus, wearied as he was from his journey"** (John 4:6) he needed a donkey to ride; therefore, he sent his disciples to bring it. **"The Lord has need of it"** (Mark 11:3)

He (PBUH) also felt upset and depressed, **"And began to be greatly distressed and troubled"** (Mark 14:33) and sometimes, he felt upset and sorrowful. **"He began to be sorrowful and troubled."** (Matt.26:37)

Crying is the habit of human beings when they face difficulty and sadness, and such was what Jesus (PBUH) did. **"Jesus wept."** (John 11:35)

The devil tried to seduce him, but could not. He took Jesus (PBUH) to a high mountain, and showed him the whole world and said to him, **"To you I will give all this authority and their glory, for it has been delivered to me, and I give it to whom I will. If you, then, will worship me, it will all be yours. And Jesus answered him, "It is written, "'You shall worship the Lord your God, and him only shall you serve."** (Luke 4:6-8)

People beat and scolded him, **"When he had said these things, one of the officers standing by struck Jesus with his hand, saying, "Is that how you answer the high priest?"** (John 18:22) but he could not defend himself except by words, because he was bound. **"So the band of soldiers and their captain and the officers of the Jews arrested Jesus and bound him."** (John 18:12).

He felt hungry, he was looking for some food, **"In the morning, as he was returning to the city, he became hungry"** (Matt. 21:18) and he was thirsty. **"Said, "I thirst."** (John 19:28) Then he ate and drank. **"They gave him a piece of broiled fish, and he took it and ate before them."** (Luke 24:42-43)

He needed the food and the drink in order to grow physically and mentally. **"And the child grew."** (Luke 2:40) **"And Jesus increased in wisdom and in stature and in favor with God and man."** (Luke 2:52) The food helped him to grow physically, and the teaching of the teachers and the elders helped him grow mentally. **"They found him in the temple, sitting among the teachers, listening to them and asking them questions."** (Luke 2:46)

We are not supposed to mention here, while talking about Allah (S.W), that eating and drinking need other human actions; micturition and defecation. (God forbid and forgive us for that)

Bringing this issue to our attention, Allah (S.W) mentions this to us in the Holy Quran. **(Christ the son of Mary was no more than an apostle; many were the apostles that passed away before him. His mother was a woman of truth. They had both to eat their (daily) food.)** (Holy Quran, 5:75).

Anyone who eats and drinks needs to excrete the waste of that food, and it is blasphemy even to think about that for Allah (S.W).

The Gospels also mention Jesus' (PBUH) sadness the eve of the crucifixion, **"My soul is very sorrowful, even to death."** (Mark 14:34) and when he was exhausted, an angel from heaven came to strengthen him. **"And there appeared to him an angel from heaven, strengthening him."** (Luke 22:43)

According to the Gospels, when he was on the cross, he was exhausted and cried, **"My God, my God, why have you forsaken me?"** (Mark 15:34)

Not only did Jesus (PBUH) do the above mentioned, but also, as the Gospels claim, he died, how could anyone imagine a dead God? **"And Jesus uttered a loud cry and breathed his last."** (Mark 15:37)

If someone tries to answer this question, saying that the dead was the human part and not the divine, and Allah (S.W) is immortal, I remind the reader, that the person who died on the cross is the Son of God and not the Son of Man. **"For God so loved the world,** that he gave his only Son, that whoever believes in him should not perish." (John 3:16)

Trying to answer this fatal question, Turtellian (third century) could not find an answer except to say, "The Son of God had died! That is incredible; because it is something unbelievable and unacceptable by the mind. He was buried with the dead; it is certain, because it should have been impossible."[1] In spite of this saying, Turtillian and Christians after him still believe that he is Allah (S.W).

The Gospels also mention Jesus' (PBUH) prayer and supplication to Allah (S.W). **"Prayed, saying, "My Father, if it be possible, let this cup pass from me; nevertheless, not as I will, but as you will".** (Matt. 26:39) **"And there he prayed"** (Mark 1:35)

Describing his prayer, Luke said, **"and knelt down and prayed"** (Luke 22:41) **"he went out to the mountain to pray, and all night he continued in prayer to God. And when day came, he called his disciples"** (Luke 6:12-13)

One may ask, to whom did Jesus (PBUH) pray all night, was he praying to himself or to the Allah (S.W) that dwells in him? Why would people leave worshipping the worshipped, to worship the worshipper?

Luke also mentioned that Jesus' sweat was like drops of blood. He says, **"And being in an agony he prayed more earnestly; and his sweat became like great drops of blood falling down to the ground. And when he rose from prayer, he came to the disciples."** (Luke 22:44) Explaining that, Yohanna Fam Ethahab said, "Who cannot be surprised, seeing God Kneeling and praying?"[2]

The description of Jesus' condition (PBUH) when he raised Lazarus, which we find in The Gospel according to John, shows his weakness and his need for Allah's (S.W) help. **"And Jesus lifted up his eyes and said, "Father, I thank you that you have heard me. I knew that you always hear me, but I said this on account of the people standing around, that they may believe that you sent me."** (John 11:41-42)

---

[1] - Christ in the Quran, the Torah and the Gospel, Abdul Kareem El Khateeb, pp 343

[2] - the frank opinion about the will and nature of Christ, Gebrial abdel Maseeh, pp 58

Prayer and worship are servants' deeds, and it is unacceptable to attribute these deeds to Allah (S.W) or to the person in whom Allah (S.W) was incarnated.

Paul mentioned Jesus' (PBUH) victory on everything including death, but he also mentioned his weaknesses and total submission to Allah (S.W). He said, **"When all things are subjected to him, then the Son himself will also be subjected to him who put all things in subjection under him, that God may be all in all."** (Co.1 15:28)

Finally, what proves that Jesus (PBUH) is human, is what he (PBUH) said regarding entering heaven, which Allah (S.W) has prepared for His faithful believers, and that he will eat and drink as his disciples, who are among those believers. **"In my Father's house are many rooms. I go to prepare a place for you. That where I am you may be also."** (John 14:2-3) **"I will not drink again of this fruit of the vine until that day when I drink it new with you in my Father's kingdom."** (Matt. 26:29)

The Kingdom of God is heaven, where he (PBUH) will meet his disciples again and he will drink with them. Is the Son going to incarnate in the Hereafter again, and what is the point of doing so, or will he be back as human and live in Allah's (S.W) heaven as all believers?

The conclusion of all the above, we take it from what Jesus (PBUH) mentioned about himself. He said, **"A man who has told you the truth that I heard from God."** (John 8:40). Should we not take his testimony (PBUH)? If he is Allah (S.W), it is not right for him to hide this fact from us by saying this plain and clear sentence, which proves that he is only human.

When Christians insist on his divinity, they are ignoring and throwing Jesus' (PBUH) and his disciples' words in the ocean, and denying all these passages, which do not speak about incarnated God nor about a human that Allah (S.W) dwells in.

Third Category

These are verses and passages, which declare Jesus' (PBUH) disciples, his contemporaries and his enemies' ignorance of the divinity concept. These verses and passages prove that neither

Jesus (PBUH) nor his disciples had anything to do with the concept of divinity, but it is an invention, which came much later after his time, and that is sufficient to refute the case.

These passages and verses are many; the following are some examples.

1- His virgin mother's (PBUH) ignorance of his divinity is one of them. While Jesus (PBUH) was going back with his mother and Joseph the carpenter, something, which proved his mother's ignorance of his divinity occurred. If his pure mother did not know of his divinity, who else would?

In the Book of Luke, we read, **"And when the feast was ended, as they were returning, the boy Jesus stayed behind in Jerusalem. His parents did not know it, but supposing him to be in the group they went a day's journey, but then they began to search for him among their relatives and acquaintances, and when they did not find him, they returned to Jerusalem, searching for him. After three days, they found him in the temple, sitting among the teachers, listening to them and asking them questions. "Son, why have you treated us so? Behold, your father and I have been searching for you in great distress."** (Luke 2:43-48). Their worries about Jesus (PBUH) were meaningless if she knew that he was Allah (S.W).

Jesus (PBUH) answered his mother's question, saying, **"Why were you looking for me? Did you not know that I must be in my Father's house?'** (Luke 2:49). Did she and Joseph understand from his words that he meant that he is Allah (S.W) or a real son of Allah (S.W)? Of course not, for they did not know anything about this strange belief. Luke says, **"And they did not understand the saying that he spoke to them."** (Luke 2:50)

When Simon carried the baby – Jesus (PBUH) – and praised Allah (S.W) because he had seen the Messiah, his mother (PBUH) heard and saw the happiness in his face. She and Joseph the Carpenter did not understand what he said and they were surprised and confused. **"And his father and his mother marveled at what was said about him."** (Luke 2:33)

2- Simon Peter, who was the dearest to Jesus (PBUH), said while he was full of the Holy Spirit, **"Men of Israel, hear these words: Jesus of Nazareth, a man attested to you by God with**

mighty works and wonders and signs that God did through him in your midst, as you yourselves know. This Jesus, delivered up according to the definite plan and foreknowledge of God, you crucified and killed by the hands of lawless men." (Acts 2:22-23) He did not mention in this important speech, supported by the Holy Spirit, anything about a divine human nor about God incarnate.

3- When Jesus (PBUH) appeared – after his assumed crucifixion- to two of his friends who were upset because of the rumors of his crucifixion, he asked them about the reason for their sadness. They said, **"Concerning Jesus of Nazareth, a man who was a prophet mighty in deed and word before God and all the people. and how our chief priests and rulers delivered him up to be condemned to death, and crucified him. But we had hoped that he was the one to redeem Israel."** (Luke 24:19-21). There is nothing in their answer about a murdered divine human, nor anything about incarnated God who had concurred death. What they saw in him was not more than a man, a savior, who was the expected Messiah of whom the prophets had foretold.

Ibrahim Saeed, an Egyptian priest, regarding these two disciples, said, "Until that moment they did not believe in his divinity… but we do not deny that they were believers of his prophethood." [1]

4- When his disciples witnessed his miracles, they were surprised. If they considered him (PBUH) Allah (S.W), there would have been no surprise in the performance of those miracles. When he passed by the fig tree and did not find any fruit on it, Jesus (PBUH) said, **"And he said to it, "May no fruit ever come from you again!" And the fig tree withered at once. When the disciples saw it, they marveled, saying, "How did the fig tree wither at once?"** (Matt. 21:18-22). Their surprise was an indication that they knew nothing of what today's Christians claim, for there is no surprise if Allah (S.W) is able to make a green tree dry.

The disciples' and Jesus' (PBUH) contemporaries did not think of him as more than the Messiah; the great-expected prophet. They did not even think of his divinity or his son-ship to Allah (S.W).

Bishop Matta El Meskeen said, "The disciples thought of him as only a prophet, but he performed deeds which no prophet had performed… that made them think of him as more than a prophet,

---

[1] - Luke's Gospel Commentary, Ibraheem Saeed, pp 634

but what was he? The disciples had collected sufficient evidence which assured them that he was the Messiah." [1]

Seeing Jesus' (PBUH) miracles, the Samaritan woman said, **""Sir, I perceive that you are a prophet."** (John 4:19) and she did not add a word. Jesus' (PBUH) reaction to her was not of any kind of scolding or correction, he did not correct her because that was what people – including his disciples- believed.

The same happened when Jesus (PBUH) cured the blind man, who witnessed Allah's (S.W) power after his eyes opened. The people asked him, **""Then how were your eyes opened? He answered, "The man called Jesus."** (John 9:10-11). However, Christians believe from this event more than that man, who confessed that Jesus (PBUH) was just a man.

The crowds, who used to see Jesus (PBUH) in Jerusalem and went to welcome him when he entered like a hero, considered him as human and a prophet. **"And the crowds said, "This is the prophet Jesus"** (Matt. 21:11)

Even his Jewish enemies thought of him the same. They were asking for a sign, but he told them that they would only see a sign like the sign of Jonah (PBUH). **"Then some of the scribes and Pharisees answered him, saying, "Teacher, we wish to see a sign from you. But he answered them, "An evil and adulterous generation seeks for a sign, but no sign will be given to it except the sign of the prophet Jonah."** (Matt. 12:38-39)

Those Jews, without doubt, were asking for a sign, proving his prophethood and not his divinity. If Jesus (PBUH) claimed divinity-- which he did not – the Jews would not accept that sign, and they would ask him to perform miracles that are greater than Jonah's and the other prophets'.

Doubting Jesus' (PBUH) prophethood, a Pharisee was watching Jesus (PBUH) while a crying sinful woman came to Jesus and cleaned his feet with her hair, kissed them and applied some perfume on them. He said, **"Now when the Pharisee who had invited him saw this, he said to himself, "If this man were a prophet, he would have known who and what sort of**

woman this is who is touching him, for she is a sinner." (Luke 7:39)

In his heart, the Pharisee denied Jesus' prophethood – not divinity- because Jesus (PBUH) did not know the identity of that woman, and that proves that he (PBUH) claimed that he is just a prophet.

In this regard, Matta El Meskeen said, "The Pharisee, when he saw that Jesus had accepted what the woman did, took it as a confession against Jesus that he was not a prophet, like the people said."[1]

In addition, the Jews wanted to kill him for they considered him a criminal, and they charged him with claiming prophethood, not divinity. They said to Nicodemus, **"Are you from Galilee too? Search and see that no prophet arises from Galilee."** (John 7:52). They accused him of lying by saying that he is a prophet, since no prophet came out of Galilee.

The devil also did not consider Jesus (PBUH) more than a man. He dared to seduce him; he took him to the mountain for forty days without food or drink-- testing, seducing and promising him the world if he would prostrate to him just one time. **"Again, the devil took him to a very high mountain and showed him all the kingdoms of the world and their glory. And he said to him, "All these I will give you, if you will fall down and worship me. Then Jesus said to him, "Be gone, Satan! For it is written, "'You shall worship the Lord your God and him only shall you serve."** (Matt. 4:8-10) Did the devil promise Allah (S.W) – who has everything and everything belongs to him – the world?

In his commentaries in Matthews's Gospel and quoting Jerome's words in this regard, priest Tadress Yaakoob Malatee, wrote, "The devil's intention of doing that was to know whether or not Jesus was truly the Son of God, but the savior was good in his answers, leaving the devil in doubt." It is clear that the devil was and remained ignorant of Jesus' (PBUH) claimed divinity.

Furthermore, if Jesus (PBUH) was Allah (S.W), how could one explain Judas' betrayal? Can anyone betray Allah (S.W)?

How can one explain Peter's denial - three times - and condemnation of Jesus (PBUH), the night of his arrest? What is said of Jesus

---

[1] - The Gospel according to Luke, Matta El Meskeen, pp331

(PBUH) as divine or God, creates many questions, which will remain without answers.

Finally, not only his contemporaries said that he was human, but also the previous prophecies, which Christians believe, affirm the same. They said that he (PBUH) has fulfilled these prophecies, but as we all know, these prophecies did not foretell about a coming God, but about a noble righteous prophet.

Fourth Category

These are verses and passages, which declare Jesus' (PBUH) prophethood, and that is more proof against his divinity.

Jesus' (PBUH) contemporaries professed of his prophethood and message, which are human characteristics and not Allah's (S.W). In the Book of John, we read, **"You call me Teacher and Lord, and you are right, for so I am."** (John 13:13). In this, Jesus (PBUH) accepted and confirmed their belief as they called him lord and master. It was common during his time to call him such, **"And he said to him, Teacher"** (Mark 10:20). Was it moral not to call him "God" and use this humble title "Master" instead?

Jesus (PBUH) started his mission as a prophet when he was thirty, **"Jesus, when he began his ministry, was about thirty years of age"** (Luke 3:23) and there was a time that the Holy Spirit had not been given to him. **"For as yet the Spirit had not been given, because Jesus was not yet glorified."** (John 7:39)

In addition, Jesus (PBUH) himself confessed that his God is one and that he is just a messenger. **"You, the only true God, and Jesus Christ whom you have sent."** (John 17:3). Similarly, he said, **"And they took offense at him. But Jesus said to them, "A prophet is not without honor except in his hometown and in his own household."** (Matt. 13:57). He considered himself like the rest of the prophets, whom are not honored among their people.

When the Pharisees threatened Jesus (PBUH) with Herod, he confirmed, once again, that he is just a prophet. He said, **"I must go on my way today and tomorrow and the day following, for it Jerusalem. O Jerusalem, Jerusalem, the city that kills the prophets and stones those who are sent to it."** (Luke 13:33-34) He confessed his prophethood and he was afraid of murder, like many other prophets; therefore, he left Jerusalem calling it 'killer of prophets' not 'Killer of Gods'.

When he (PBUH) performed his miracles, he used to pray to Allah (S.W), linking his miracles to his message and prophethood. **"But I said this on account of the people standing around, that they may believe that you sent me."** (John 11:42)

When the Jews tried to kill him once, he made a statement, in which he made a clear confession that he is human and just a messenger of Allah (S.W). **"But now you seek to kill me, a man who has told you the truth that I heard from God."** (John 8:40).

Confirming that, he told his disciples many times that he is a messenger, and his words are infallible, for he speaks with inspiration from Allah (S.W). **"Jesus said to them again, "Peace be with you. As the Father has sent me, even so I am sending you."** (John 20:21)

He affirmed that again, when he said, **"the Father who sent me has himself given me a commandment--what to say and what to speak"** (John 12:49) and he said, **"the word that you hear is not mine but the Father's who sent me."** (John 14:24)

"My teaching is not mine, but his who sent me." (John 7:16) he also said, **"Nor is a messenger greater than the one who sent him."** (John 13:16)

That everyone during his time believed in him as a prophet, and confronting him with that, without his objection, is another confirmation that he (PBUH) was just a prophet. **"Fear seized them all, and they glorified God, saying, "A great prophet has arisen among us!" and "God has visited his people!"** (Luke 7:16) and when he fed the crowd with the five loaves and two fish, people said, **""This is indeed the Prophet who is to come into the world!"** (John 6:14) even Paul, **"for there is one God, and there is one mediator between God and men, the man Christ Jesus."** (Tim.1 2:5)

In his book 'The Spreading Universe' Sir Arthur Findlay was right. He said, "Jesus was not God or savior, but he was a messenger of God who served, during his short life, to cure the sick and to tell news about the hereafter. He taught that life in this world is just a preparation for the Kingdom of God, which is a better life for every righteous."

From the above, we see the proof that Jesus (PBUH) was a servant of Allah (S.W), and great messenger from Him, which is identical to the Muslims belief. **"He was no more than a servant: We granted Our favour to him, and We made him an example to the Children of Israel."** (Holy Quran 43:59)

THE PURPOSE OF INCARNATION

Christians believe that Allah (S.W) was incarnated in Jesus (PBUH), and their evidence for that is what comes in the Gospel according to John. **"And the Word became flesh and dwelt among us."** (John 1:14)

To understand this passage, we read what the Monastic Jesuits Edition's scholars said regarding the incarnation of the wisdom, which is in Proverbs (8:22). They said, "The idea of the incarnated wisdom, which is just a literature art as in Proverbs (14:1), was developed in Israel at the time of the captivity; when worshipping idols ceased to be a threat to the right religion. In all passages that mention the incarnation of the wisdom, the word or the spirit, it is difficult to distinguish between the poetic art, the old religious belief and the new inspiration."

Thus, it is possible that the passage, which speaks of the word incarnation, is just a literature art, which is the same as the metaphoric incarnation of the wisdom, when it went out, **"Wisdom cries aloud in the street, in the markets she raises her voice; at the head of the noisy streets she cries out."** (Pro. 1:20-21) and considering ignorance as a wild woman. (Pro. 9:13-18)[1]

In this regard, scholars are asking about the reason for the incarnation of the Son and why it is not the Father's or the Holy Spirit's incarnation. They also ask why Allah (S.W) had to incarnate into a human figure: come down from His high throne, enter the womb of a woman and finally, be born from her.

Clergymen have been working hard to answer these questions, and when they did not find any answer in their books, they used their thoughts. Consequently, they have different opinions, and as they cannot find proof for Paul's claim of God's incarnation, they also cannot find a reason for that incarnation.

Their answers and conclusions are as follows:

First: This is a mystery, which we cannot understand, but we have to believe.

Second: The incarnation is to fill the gap between Allah (S.W) and humanity, and to reconcile it with seeing Allah (S.W).

---

[1]- See also, (Sirach 4:11, Proverbs 9:1-6, 23:23) and other passages.

Third: The incarnation is a way to make people return to Allah (S.W) and worship Him and to leave the worship of idols and other creations; therefore, Allah (S.W) incarnated Himself into a human figure in order to be worshipped. Saint Ephraim said, "God saw us (humans) worshipping idols and creations, that is why He wore a created body to hunt us to worship Him."[1]

Fourth: The incarnation is necessary to reconcile Allah's (S.W) justice and His mercy, for His justice ordained the death of humans and His mercy ordained that they live; for that, Jesus (PBUH) was the sacrifice.

Regarding that, Ethanasius, who was one of the most important people on the Nicene Council, said, "That is why the word of God had to bring forth the sinful man to righteousness. At the same time, fulfill what the father requires, and since he – Jesus- is God's word, he was the only suitable one, who can renew everything and bear the pain instead of everyone else before the father. For that, he came down to our world without body, clean and without sin. He did bear the pain of death in order to prevent the death of humans, because then his father's creation would be a waste. He took a body like our bodies. If he did not come and dwell among us, then that would be the end of the human race."

Did Jesus' death (PBUH) change the death issue for humans, or do people still die until now?

Answering this question, Ethanasius said, "Death entered this world by the devil's envy. After that, people started to sin and to die; the devil had authority more than it was supposed, because he came as a result of God's threat in the case of sin."

I wonder what death's natural authority is, and I wonder what is the difference between people's death before and after Jesus (PBUH). One has the right to ask, what is the secret about death taking other creatures' lives?

Ethanasius also mentioned another reason for Allah's (S.W) incarnation, which is to comfort humans. He said, "When God, the controller of everything, created humans by His word and saw their weaknesses in knowing God or even having a concept of Him, He came down to show them Himself. He did not leave them without

---

[1]- The frank opinion about the will and the nature of Christ, bishop Ghebrial Abdel Maseeh, pp 59

knowledge of Him, in order to prevent them thinking that their existence is useless."[1]

According to this, the reason for Allah's (S.W) incarnation is for humankind to know their God and to destroy the gap between the Creator and the creation. This is what Snout mentioned in his book "The Original Christianity", as he said, "there is an endless big gap, …. In addition, if God did not begin and amend the matter, it would remain the same. Humans would be hopeless, wondering, but God spoke and declared Himself." [2]

Dr Abdul Karim Al Khateeb wonders, "How was the relation between the prophets and their God with such a gap?

Did they know their God with sufficient knowledge, which led them to worship and obey Him?

Was their faith in Allah (S.W) weak and untrue?

What changes happened to humankind after Allah's (S.W) incarnation? Did all people believe in Allah (S.W) and know Him? Did Atheism disappear from the world?"

What kind of pleasure is there for humanity in seeing their God slapped, beaten, and whipped? This reduces every belief about Allah (S.W) in their minds, as humans are created with eagerness and curiosity longing to know the invisible; the unseen things. If they know about it, if the unknown was revealed, there would be no more longing, their desire would be less towards the thing they were looking for and searching for so hard.

What about the other generations, who did not have the pleasure of seeing the incarnated God? Would it be fair to exclude them? How could they know their God if they did not see Him?

Why was our pleasure and comfort in seeing Allah (S.W) in His childhood and His youth, but not in His middle and old age?

Muslims refuse these justifications, which offend the greatness of Allah (S.W), make Him incapable of forgiveness, and make Him confused between His mercy and His justice. Such issues do not occur with wise people, how could we accept them for Allah (S.W)?

---

[1] - Christ in the Quran, The Torah and the Gospel, Abdul Kareem el Khateeb, pp 158-160
[2] - ibid, 130-132, 160-170

These justifications make Allah (S.W) unable to guide people to worship Him except in a polytheistic way that they know.

Charles Gene Pier has the same opinion - he agrees in the weakness of these justifications. He affirms that Paul was the one who created the idea of the incarnated God. He explains the reasons, which led Paul to do that. Paul came up with the incarnation idea after realizing that "the new polytheist followers will not accept the crucifixion scandal, and, there must be a good explanation for Jesus' shameful death, which the enemy did not stop from relating matters to it. That explanation must be sufficient to make the crucifixion event an event of deep religious significance.

Paul (the apostle) dealt with this problem… he developed a solution, which had a huge influence; he ignored the idea of Jesus of Nazareth, which was the major concept of the twelve. He mentioned nothing but the crucified Jesus, imagining him as a divine character, who existed before the world itself and considered him as a kind of personification. The apostle found the basic elements of secrets; he found them without even looking for them…"[1]

Paul faced another difficulty while he was finishing the crucified incarnated God, and that was, what was he going to say about Jesus' death on the cross, since the Torah states that every crucified person is cursed? (Deuteronomy 21:23), Thus, this shameful death was an insult to Jesus, and made him cursed according to the Jewish Law.

To solve this fatal matter, Paul decided to make the cursed as an example of sacrifice, and make him God, who descended and incarnated to redeem humans' sins. He became a curse to redeem them from the Law's curse, as Paul says, **"but God shows his love for us in that while we were still sinners, Christ died for us. Since, therefore, we have now been justified by his blood, much more shall we be saved by him from the wrath of God. For if while we were enemies we were reconciled to God by the death of his Son."** (Romans 5:8-10), he became a curse to save us from the Law's curse. [1]

Finally, what Christians say about Allah (S.W), multiplicity and incarnation, is a kind of a human trifling, and a clear insult on Allah (S.W). The sculptor, as the guided Mohammad Majdi Murjan said,

---

[1] - Christianity, its beginning and its development, Charles Gene Pier, pp 134

[1] - People of the Book, Let Us Come to a Common Term, Raoof Shalaby, pp 265

"When he makes a statue he can destroy it, and no one can say that the statue will claim that it was made of the same substance as its maker, or that it is part of him.

The powerless human, who is one of Allah's (S.W) creations, dared to insult his Creator; he became arrogant and ignorant, and then turned these facts upside down. He reformed his Maker, and, from his own imagination, divided Him into three parts, making each part as God, consequently, transferring the one and only God into three. He also divided the work and the burden on his three gods, which he did to pity the one God so as not to carry all these burdens alone by Himself. How miserable is man!"[1]

In fact, the idea of incarnation is one of the most important reasons for the spread of Atheism among Christians. Human beings tend to glorify and esteem their Creator by their own spirits and instincts, and consider Him the most adorable and far above being equal to anyone; Christianity, all the while, makes Allah (S.W) as a human, who came from the womb of an Israeli woman.

Cranes Airsold said, "From the scientific point of view, I cannot imagine God materially, who can be seen or replaced anywhere"[2]

Consequently, people face difficulty in choosing between the wrong belief and the true instinct, which their minds support. Many of them find no alternative other than to disbelieve in the church that whipped and crucified God, which increases Atheism. Allah (S.W) is far above what they say.

One of the disadvantages of the incarnation creed is that it weakens the morals and principles that Jesus taught and made him a good example for his followers. The call of Jesus' (PBUH) divinity affects all that, as people cannot follow and do what Allah (S.W) has done.

The writers of The Encyclopedia Americana said, "If Jesus was God, then the morals and principles, which he performed and gave to us during his humble life, would be invaluable, as he has power which we do not have, and humans cannot imitate God."

In his book "on Jesus steps" Tomas Ecembesphy said, "If Jesus was God, then one cannot follow him and follow his tradition.

---

[1] - God Almighty One or Three, Mohammad Majdy Morjan, pp125
[2] - Monotheistic Christians in History, Ahmad Abdul Wahab, pp 38-39, 45

THE DIVINITY OF THE HOLY SPIRIT

The Holy Spirit, for Muslims, is a name for the angel Gabriel (PBUH), and a name for Allah's (S.W) inspiration and His support for his prophets.

The Holy Quran calls the angel Gabriel (PBUH) as the Holy Spirit. Allah (S.W) Says, **"Say, the Holy Spirit has brought the revelation from thy Lord in Truth"** (Holy Quran 16:102), also, Allah (S.W) says, **"Then will Allah say: "O Jesus the son of Mary! Recount My favour to thee and to thy mother. Behold! I strengthened thee with the holy spirit."** (Holy Quran 5:110)

In addition, the Holy Quran calls Allah's (S.W) inspiration to his prophets as Spirit. Allah (S.W) says, **"And thus have We, by Our Command, sent inspiration to thee."** (Holy Quran 42:52), He also says, **"Raised high above ranks (or degrees), (He is) the Lord of the Throne (of Authority): by His Command doth He send the Spirit (of inspiration) to any of His servants he pleases."** (Holy Quran 40:15)

It is important to mention, that what the Holy Quran says about the Holy Spirit is not far from what the Bible says, but it does not agree with the Constantinople Council meaning.

The Holy Bible mentions that various creatures hold the name 'Holy Spirit':

1- The human spirit, which Allah (S.W) creates in his creations, is Allah's (S.W) Spirit, which He creates in them. **"And to the spirits of the righteous made perfect."** (Heb. 12/23), **"when you take away their breath, they die and return to their dust. When you send forth your Spirit, they are created, and you renew the face of the ground."** (Psalms 104/29-30) Allah (S.W) gave life to Adam by the same spirit. **"and breathed into his nostrils the breath of life, and the man became a living creature."** (Gen. 2/7). This spirit is called 'the spirit of Allah (S.W)' because it came from Allah (S.W), and to Him it will return. **"And the spirit returns to God who gave it."** (Ecc. 12/7).

2- The inspiration that the angels carry to prophets, **"David himself, in the Holy Spirit, declared"** (Mark 12/36), also

"And his father Zechariah was filled with the Holy Spirit" (Luke 1/67), Peter said, **"Brothers, the Scripture had to be fulfilled, which the Holy Spirit spoke beforehand by the mouth of David."** (Acts 1/16). Allah (S.W) called the prophets and what they bring of this inspiration as the Holy Spirit, as He said scolding the people of Israel, **"You stiff-necked people, uncircumcised in heart and ears, you always resist the Holy Spirit. As your fathers did, so do you. Which of the prophets did not your fathers persecute?"** (Acts 7/51-52)

3- The Holy Spirit is also a name for the aid and wisdom, which Allah (S.W) gives to His prophets and others, and the angels or others can deliver it. Jesus said, **"But if it is by the Spirit of God that I cast out demons."** (Matt. 12:28) and what Pharaoh said to his servants, when he was looking for a wise man. **"Can we find a man like this, in whom is the Spirit of God?"** (Gen. 41/38) **"Now there was a man in Jerusalem, whose name was Simeon, and this man was righteous and devout, waiting for the consolation of Israel, and the Holy Spirit was upon him."** (Luke 2/25), also, the Holy Spirit supported the disciples on the fiftieth day **"And they were all filled with the Holy Spirit and began to speak in other tongues as the Spirit gave them utterance."** (Acts 2/4). This is the same as what the prophet Haggai said, **"My Spirit remains in your midst. Fear not."** (Haggai 2/5)

4- The strong wind also called the Holy Spirit. Describing the destroying wind, the Torah says, **"The grass withers, the flower fades when the breath of the LORD blows on it."** (Isaiah 40/7), the same is in Genesis, **"And the Spirit of God was hovering over the face of the waters."** (Gen. 1/2), there is a mistranslation in this passage that leads to this confusion. The passage, as the great critic Espinoza said, 'means a strong wind came from God, and ceased darkness.'

Moreover, relating the spirit to Allah (S.W) in the last two passages is glorification and esteem, not deifying, as it says, **"The mountains of God"** (Psalms 36/6)

Those who worship the Holy Spirit do not accept all the meanings that I have mentioned. They do not accept the idea that the Holy Spirit is just a power or angel from Allah (S.W). The Holy Spirit, according to the Christian concept is God, is the third hypostasis of the Trinity. What is the Holy Spirit according to their concept? What evidence do they have for considering him as a God? When did that happen?

In 381 C.E, by the order of the Emperor Tedious, the Council of Constantinople formed, to discuss Bishop Macedonius' belief. He denied the divinity of the Holy Spirit; and he believed what the Holy Books mentioned about him. He believed that, "The Holy Spirit is a divine work spread in the world, not a divine person who is different from the Father and the Son", and, "He is like all the creations", and he saw him as a servant of the Son just like one of the angels.

One hundred and fifty priests attended this council. These priests decided to deprive Macedonius of his office, and they made one important decision never made by the church councils before, which was deifying the Holy Spirit. They considered him as a complement to the Trinity. They said, "We have no other meaning for the Holy Spirit except the Spirit of God, God is nothing except his life, and saying that the Holy Spirit is a creation, is the same as saying that God is a creation." [1]

Priest Yasin Mansor said, "The Holy Spirit is the eternal God, he existed before the creation, and he is the creator of everything, able to do anything. He is present everywhere, and he is the everlasting and the unlimited".

He also said, "The Holy Spirit is the third hypostasis of the Trinity. He is not just a power or characteristic, but a real self, a living person, and a distinct divine being. He is not separate; he is a divine unit different from the Father and the Son, but equal to them in power and position, sharing with them the basic and the same divinity.[2]

Christians refer to John's Gospel when talking about the divinity of the Holy Spirit: **"God is spirit"** (John 4/24). They also believe that he is the spirit that existed from the beginning of creation, **"In the beginning, God created the heavens and the earth. The Spirit of God was hovering over the face of the waters."** (Genesis 1/1-2). Many other passages also mention spirit, God spirit, or the Holy Spirit.

---

[1]- People of the Book, Let Us Come to a Common Term, Raoof Shalaby, pp 218 -221
[2] - Christian Hypostasis, Ahmad Hejazy Assaqa, pp 42-44. Allah One or Three, Mohammad Magdy Morjan, pp 116 - 125

Refuting Christian Evidence for the Divinity of the Holy Spirit

I suppose that what I have mentioned about the meaning of the Holy Spirit in the Holy Bible is enough to disprove this strange belief. Moreover, the meaning of the words "the Holy Spirit", which Christians believe, does not exist in the Holy Bible. If we attentively study the passages, which mention the Holy Spirit, we will be certain about the strangeness of this belief.

The Holy Spirit incarnated itself into different images - one as a pigeon, which descended on Jesus (PBUH) while he was praying, **"and the Holy Spirit descended on him in bodily form, like a dove"** (Luke 3/22). Was that pigeon Allah (S.W)?

At another time, it came as fiery tongues, when it overshadowed the disciples on the fiftieth day. **"And suddenly there came from heaven a sound like a mighty rushing wind, and it filled the entire house where they were sitting. And divided tongues as of fire appeared to them and rested on each one of them. And they were all filled with the Holy Spirit."** (Acts 2/2-4)

Why do Christians not accept that the Holy Spirit could be Gabriel (PBUH) or Allah's (S.W) angel as mentioned in their Holy Book? The Holy Spirit came to Cornelius and Peter, and he was one of Allah's (S.W) angels **"the Spirit said to him, "Behold, three men are looking for you. Rise and go down and accompany them without hesitation, for I have sent them. And Peter went down to the men.... And they said, Cornelius.... Was directed by a holy angel to send for you to come to his house and to hear what you have to say."** (Acts 10/20-22) The Holy angel was the Spirit that spoke to Peter and it was he, who asked Cornelius to send his men to Peter.

The enemy of the Israelites from among the angels is Gabriel (PBUH). He is the Holy Spirit who saved them many times, then when they insisted on disbelieving, he became angry with them, tutored them, and became their enemy. **"And the angel of his presence saved them; in his love and in his pity he redeemed them; he lifted them up and carried them all the days of old. But they rebelled and grieved his Holy Spirit; therefore he turned to be their enemy, and himself fought against them."** (Isaiah 63/9-10) They upset Allah's (S.W) Holy Spirit, the angel, thus, turning his love to enmity.

The Holy Spirit was with the people of Israel when they left Egypt. **"Then he remembered the days of old, of Moses and his people. Where is he who brought them up out of the sea with the shepherds of his flock? Where is he who put in the midst of them his Holy Spirit, Who divided the waters before them to make for himself an everlasting name."** (Isaiah 63/11), but he was an angel not a divine person. **"Behold, I send an angel before you to guard you on the way and to bring you to the place that I have prepared."** (Exodus 23/20) The Holy Spirit is the angel that was with them.

Allah's (S.W) Spirit is not a name for Gabriel, but it is the name for many other angels as well. **"And between the throne and the four living creatures and among the elders I saw a Lamb standing, as though it had been slain, with seven horns and with seven eyes, which are the seven spirits of God sent out into all the earth."** (Revelation 5/6). The Spirits that John saw were not gods; otherwise the Christian Trinity would not be a threesome, but a ten-some.

Revelation mentions these seven Spirits of Allah (S.W) in two other places: **"From the throne came flashes of lightning, and rumblings and peals of thunder, and before the throne were burning seven torches of fire, which are the seven spirits of God."** (Revelation 4/5), **"And to the angel of the church in Sardis write: 'The words of him who has the seven spirits of God and the seven stars."** (Revelation 3/1).

Whoever the Holy Spirit is, he is not Allah (S.W). If he is God, he should do everything by himself, but he cannot. Peter said, **"But men spoke from God as they were carried along by the Holy Spirit."** (Peter (2) 1/21). If the Holy Spirit were an everlasting God and equal to the Father in every thing, he would make people speak his own words.

What disproves the divinity of the Holy Spirit is his ignorance – just like others - of the time of the Day of Judgment, as no one knows it except the Father. **"But concerning that day or that hour, no one knows, not even the angels in heaven, nor the Son, but only the Father."** (Mark 13/32)

Another fact disproving the Holy Spirit's divinity is that the passages speak of him as a gift from Allah (S.W) to men, as Jesus said, **"If you then, who are evil, know how to give good gifts to your** children, how much more will the heavenly Father give the Holy Spirit to those who ask him!"** (Luke 11/13). It does not make sense that Allah (S.W), as the third divine being, is a gift that is given to and owned by people.

Moreover, if the Holy Spirit is God, we should consider the people who he descended on, as God. He descended on many people, like David, **"And I will dwell among the children of Israel and will not forsake my people Israel."** (Kings (1) 6/13); Simon, **"Now there was a man in Jerusalem, whose name was Simeon, and this man was righteous and devout, waiting for the consolation of Israel, and the Holy Spirit was upon him."**(Luke 2/25); the disciples, **"But you will receive power when the Holy Spirit has come upon you, and you will be my witnesses."** (Acts 1/8). Finally, he descended on the people of Corinth, who believed in Paul. Paul said, **"Do you not know that your body is a temple of the Holy Spirit within you?"** (Corinthians (1) 6/19). All these are worth worshipping if God – the Holy Spirit - is in them and fills them.

Not only does the Holy Bible consider those who believe in the Holy Spirit as believers, but it also considers the same for people who do not hear of the Holy Spirit. In addition, it considers them as disciples even though they do not know this claimed God. **"And it happened that while Apollos was at Corinth, Paul passed through the inland country and came to Ephesus. There he found some disciples. And he said to them, "Did you receive the Holy Spirit when you believed?" And they said, "No, we have not even heard that there is a Holy Spirit."** (Acts 19/1-2) This, without doubt, disproves the divinity of the Holy Spirit.

What Christians refer to, regarding the divinity of the Holy Spirit in **"God is spirit"** (John 4/24), is wrong. The passage does not tell about the nature of Allah (S.W), but about one of His characteristics, as in **"God is love"** (John (1) 4/16), **"God is light"** (John (1) 1/5)

John meant that no one could see God almighty, because He is not a material body of flesh and blood, and Luke affirmed this as he said, **"For a spirit does not have flesh and bones."** (Luke 24/39) supported this meaning. Answering the question: 'why do people say that God is a Spirit?', they answer, "It is said that he is a Spirit because he is far above materiality and cannot be decayed." [1]

Therefore, scholars believe that the Holy Spirit is not God, and the concept of the Trinity is a fabricated creed; made by the church councils according to the popes' and the emperors' wishes, without referring to any evidence proving this belief. A belief of which the prophets had never heard, was never mentioned by Jesus, and was unknown to the disciples.

The Modern Catholic encyclopedia was right in saying that "making one God into three persons was not established in Christian life or in their belief before the end of the fourth century."[2]

---

[1] - Explanation of the Basic of Belief, Dr. Priest Andrew Watson and Dr. Priest Ibraheem Saeed, pp 28
[2] - Forgiveness Between Islam and Christianity, Ibraheem Khaleel Ahmad, pp 95

<u>CHRISTIAN EVIDENCE OF THE TRINITY</u>

It is common, when talking about the most important creed in Christianity, which is the Trinity, to find evidence for it in many passages uttered by the prophets, then Jesus (PBUT) and his disciples after him.

However, looking attentively at the Holy Bible, we cannot find the clear evidence that we are looking for, in the Old or the New Testaments. It is incorrect to judge hastily. Let us read what the Holy Bible mentions regarding this important belief.

First: The Torah Passages and the Trinity

Christians refer to some of the Torah passages and claim that they are divine signs of the Trinity. One of these passages uses the plural Hebrew word 'Eloheem' when talking about Allah (S.W). **"In the beginning, God created the heavens and the earth."** (Genesis 1/1). Likewise, it uses what refers to plurality for the deeds that were done by Allah (S.W): **"Come, let us go down and there confuse their language."** (Genesis 11/7)

There are other passages, which Christians refer to as signs of the Trinity in the Torah. The angels' saying: **"Holy, holy, holy is the LORD of hosts."** (Isaiah 6/3) mentions the word (Holy) three times. Likewise, the animals, which John saw in his revelation said, **"Holy, holy, holy, is the Lord God Almighty"** (Revelation 4/8)

A Critique of the Passages of the Torah

Christians admit there is nothing in those passages that is clear evidence of the Trinity, which the clear monotheistic passages refute. On the other hand, the readers of the Old Testament, starting from the early prophets to the children of Israel, did not understand that these passages, as Christians claim, are indications to the Trinity.

Priest Potter admits that, saying, "After God created the world, and completed it by creating human beings, for some time he did not declare anything about Himself except monotheism, as mentioned in the Torah. However, there are still many signs behind this monotheism, because if you read attentively you will find sentences such as, (God's word), (God's wisdom), (God's spirit). Those, to whom the Torah was sent, knew about the intended meaning only from the Gospel... as, what the Torah hinted, the Gospel declared and explained." [1]

One wonders, why did Allah (S.W) conceal the Trinity from Moses (PBUH) and the Israelites? Why did He deceive them with many monotheistic passages, which made them rebel against the Trinity and deny it? Will He forgive them and others, for not finding the real meaning in these puzzles?

Scholars thought about the Christians' claim, found it deceitful, unacceptable by intelligent minds, and it does not fit with the real meaning of the context. What these passages indicate are multiple gods, without specification of three or four.

The plurals mentioned in the Torah, (Eloheem, Let us, we descend, etc.) are for glorification, as nations are accustomed to talk of their great people using plural verbs. One may say, "we, we believe, we ordered", meaning himself. The listener understands that he is talking about himself, and not himself and others.

It is common to use plurality for glorification, even in the Holy Bible. There are many examples, such as the woman, the fortune-teller, who saw Samuel's spirit after his death; she talked about him using the plural form. The Torah says, **"When the woman saw Samuel, she cried out with a loud voice. And the woman said to Saul, "I saw gods ascending out of the earth." He said to her, "What is his appearance?" And she said, "An old man is coming up, and he is wrapped in a robe." And Saul knew that it was Samuel."** (Samuel (1) 28/12-14 KJV). She was talking about Samuel, and even though she saw him as an old man, she talked of him in the plural (gods). Thus plurality does not necessarily indicate multiple numbers; it means glorification.

When the Children of Israel worshipped the calf, it was one, which the Torah mentions as plural three times. **"And he received the gold from their hand and fashioned it with a graving tool and made a golden calf. And they said, "These are your gods, O Israel, who brought you up out of the land of**

---

[1]- "Speeches on Christianity, Mohammad Abu Zahra, pp 121", "Christian Creeds between the Quran and Reason, Hashem Jodah, pp 129-130"

Egypt!" **They have made for themselves a golden calf and have worshiped it and sacrificed to it and said, 'These are your gods, O Israel, who brought you up out of the land of Egypt!"** (Exodus 32/4-8)

This chapter continues to reassure us that using the plural means one. **"So Moses returned to the LORD and said, "Alas, this people have sinned a great sin. They have made for themselves gods of gold."** (Exodus 32/31)

Simlarly, we find this plurality in the Holy Quran, as Allah (S.W) says, **"We have, without doubt, sent down the Message; and We will assuredly guard it (from corruption)."** (Holy Quran 15: 9). "We" refers to the One and Only, Allah (S.W).

Repeating words three times, as the angels and the animals, which John saw, cannot be evidence in any way. If we continue to use them as evidence, we will find many gods.

The Holy Bible mentions the word, (holy) three times twice; it also mentions it forty times as one word. This repetition is for reassurance only, as in many passages of the Gospels and the Torah.[1]

In one of these passages, the Jews say: **"but they kept shouting, "Crucify, crucify him!"** (Luke 23/21). The same also happened when Jesus (PBUH) asked Peter, he repeated it three times: **"When they had finished breakfast, Jesus said to Simon Peter, "Simon, son of John, do you love me more than these?" He said to him, "Yes, Lord; you know that I love you...He said to him a second time, "Simon, son of John, do you love me?".... He said to him the third time, "Simon, son of John, do you love me?" Peter was grieved because he said to him the third time, "Do you love me?"** (John 21/15-17).

The Gospels' Passages and the Trinity

Christians believe there is much evidence of the Trinity in the New Testament, which is much clearer than that mentioned in the Torah. They present passages such as: **"And when Jesus was baptized, immediately he went up from the water, and**

---

[1]- (Jeremiah 7:4, 22:29) (Ezekiel 21:27)

behold, the heavens were opened to him, and he saw the Spirit of God descending like a dove and coming to rest on him. And behold, a voice from heaven said, "This is my beloved Son, with whom I am well pleased."** (Matthew 3/16-17)

This passage contains the Father, the beloved Son, and the Spirit that descended in the shape of a dove. In another passage Paul said, **"The grace of the Lord Jesus Christ and the love of God and the fellowship of the Holy Spirit be with you all."** (Corinthians (2) 13/14).

Whoever reads Matthew's passage attentively, will find three selves, different in names and acts. Each of them has a different self-being; one came out from the water after baptism, the second descended as a dove, and the third is in the sky saying, (this is my beloved son). How can one say, after all this, that they are only one being?

Moreover, Christians believe that Jesus is the Son. Here the passage indicates that the spirit is incarnated in Jesus (PBUH), and assures that in many places, (Luke 3/22, Matthew 12/18) while other passages indicate that the Father is incarnated in him. (John 17/21, 14/9-10). Then which divine hypostasis is incarnated in Jesus (PBUH)?

The Holy Bible does not mention the three hypostasis of the Trinity together, except in two passages: the passage of the three witnesses in John's First Epistle, and the end of Matthew's Gospel.

A. The Passage of the Three Witnesses

The following is the more important of the two passages, of which I have spoken. John's First Epistle says: **"For there are three that testify: The Spirit, the water, and the blood-and these three are one."** (John (1) 5/7-8 International standard version).

This passage clearly shows that the three are only one God. However, it does not exist in all the old manuscripts of the Holy Bible, nor does it exist in the first printed book. It was added later.

Christian scholars admit adding it. Among them, Heron, the collectors of Henry Weskit Commentary, Adam Clark, and Fender. In addition, Saint Eckstein, when he debated in the fourth century with those who were against the Trinity, did not mention this passage. Moreover, he wrote ten dissertations commenting on John's Epistle, but he did not mention this passage.

The Revised Standard Version and some universal translations deleted it from its English version. It still exists in most of the other translations, such as Douay-Rheims Bible, the International Standard Version, James Murdock New Testament, and the Modern King James Version.

The passage in the English Standard Version and some other translations is: **"because the Spirit is the truth. For there are three that testify: the Spirit, the water and the blood; and these three agree"** (John (1) 5/6-8). The Monastic Jesuit Translation mentioned, in its introduction, the reason for the deletion. It says, "This passage was never mentioned in the manuscript before the fifteenth century or in the old ones, neither in the best Latin translations. Most likely, it was a comment written in the margin, and then was inserted into the text while in use in the west."

Benjamin Wilson, the translator of the Greek manuscripts, said the same. He said, "This sentence, which is evidence of the divinity, is not found in any of the Greek manuscripts before the fifteenth century. None of the Greek writers nor did any of the ancient Latin popes ever mention it, even when it was necessary for the topic; therefore, frankly, it is a fabrication".[1]

B- The Last Verses of Matthew's Gospel

The second passage, which Christians consider as evidence of the Trinity, is Matthew's verse in his last chapter. This verse speaks of Jesus (PBUH) before his ascent to heaven, as he gave his command to his disciples. **"And Jesus came and said to them, "All authority in heaven and on earth has been given to me. Go therefore and make disciples of all nations, baptizing them in the name of the Father and of the Son and of the Holy Spirit, teaching them to observe all that I have commanded**

---

[1]- The Truth Revealed, Rahmatullah al Hindi, Vol.2 pp 497-504. Christ (PBUH) Between Facts and Imagination, Mohammad Wasfi, pp 106-107. Fifty Thousand Errors in the Holy Bible, Ahmad Deedat, pp 12

you. And behold, I am with you always, to the end of the age." (Matthew 28/18-20)

The first critical point in this passage is, although it is a very important one, the other three Gospels do not mention it. These Gospels agree that Jesus (PBUH) entered Jerusalem riding on a donkey. Was his riding on a donkey more important than the Trinity, which no one mentioned except Matthew?

In addition, at the end of Mark's Gospel, when Jesus (PBUH) gave the command to the disciples, he did not mention the Trinity. Mark said, **"And he said to them, "Go into all the world and proclaim the gospel to the whole creation. Whoever believes and is baptized will be saved, but whoever does not believe will be condemned."** (Mark 16/15-16). That indicates the fabrication of the Trinity passage in Matthew's Gospel and shows that it is not genuine.

Moreover, this passage is a fabrication, as western scholars confirm. Wills said, "There is no proof that the apostles believed in the Trinity."

Adolph Harnack said, "The Trinity passage, which talks about the Father, the Son, and the Holy Spirit, is a strange issue to Jesus and it was not mentioned by him, and never existed in the Apostles' time. Only in the later teachings of Christianity, do we find that Jesus was giving instructions after his resurrection, for, Paul knew nothing about that."[1] (Paul did not quote Jesus' saying, which called for the spreading of Christianity among nations.)

When the historian Eusebius quoted this passage, he did not mention the Father or the Holy Spirit, but said, "they went to all nations to preach about the Gospel, relying on Jesus' power, who said to them: 'go, and teach all nations by my name'."[2]

Moreover, what assures us is that the newly discovered Hebrew manuscripts for Matthew's Gospel, which were originally written in Hebrew, do not contain this passage. This, according to Dr. G. Recart, a theology professor in the Anglican Missionary College, is strong evidence that the passage is a fabrication. He said, "Indeed,

---

[1]- Christianity Without Christ, Kamel Saafan, pp 66. Christ in Christian Creeds Resources, Ahmad Abdul Wahab, pp 61. Monotheistic Christians' Creeds Between Islam and Christianity, Husni Al Ateer, pp 92
[2]- History of the Church, Eusebius, pp 100

the Catholic Church and the Eastern Orthodox have lied to the world regarding the last verses in Matthew, for, anyone who was baptized in this way, had a wrong baptism and died without salvation." [1]

Dr. Recart also reminds us of many other passages that speak of the baptism by Jesus Christ only, as what comes in Peter's famous speech. Peter said, **""Repent and be baptized every one of you in the name of Jesus Christ for the forgiveness of your sins, and you will receive the gift of the Holy Spirit."** (Acts 2:38).

The Samaritans were baptizing by the baptism of John the Baptist, when they heard Peter, **"They were baptized in the name of the Lord Jesus."** (Acts 19:5) Peter did not ask them to baptize by the name of the Father and the Holy Spirit. [2]

The history of the disciples assures us that they did not know about that passage. They did not go to preach to all people as Jesus told them in that claimed passage. On the contrary, he told them to avoid preaching anyone other than the Jews. **"These twelve Jesus sent out, instructing them, "Go nowhere among the Gentiles and enter no town of the Samaritans. but go rather to the lost sheep of the house of Israel."** (Matthew 10/5-6).

This corresponds with a second century historical testimony, which contradicts the command of preaching to the nations and contradicts baptizing them with the Trinity. Apollonius, the historian, said, "I have received from the elders that Jesus, before ascending to heaven, commanded his disciples not to go far from Jerusalem for twelve years." [3]

The disciples followed what Jesus (PBUH) said. They did not leave Jerusalem until circumstances forced them to leave. **"Now those who were scattered because of the persecution that arose over Stephen traveled as far as Phoenicia and Cyprus and Antioch, speaking the word to no one except Jews."** (Acts 11/19).

If the disciples had heard Jesus (PBUH) commanding them to preach to all nations by the name of the Father, the Son, and the

---

[1] - www.jesus-messiah.com/apologetics/catholic/matthew-proof.html

[2] - See also, (Acts 10:48, 8:16)

[3] -Monotheistic Christians' Creeds Between Islam and Christianity, Husni Al Ateer, pp 230. Monotheistic Christians in History, Ahmad Abdul Wahab, pp 91-94

Holy Spirit, they would follow what he said willingly, and preach his message to the gentiles.

When the idolatrous Cornelius, after his conversion to Christianity by Peter, called Peter to know about Christianity, the disciples blamed Peter for doing so. Then Peter said to them, **"You yourselves know how unlawful it is for a Jew to associate with or to visit anyone of another nation, but God has shown me that I should not call any person common or unclean."** (Acts 10/28).

We notice here that Peter did not mention that Jesus (PBUH) asked them to do so, but he said **"to us who had been chosen by God as witnesses, who ate and drank with him after he rose from the dead. And he commanded us to preach to the people."** (Acts 10/41-42), meaning the Jews only.

When he returned to Jerusalem, he faced more blame. **"So when Peter went up to Jerusalem, the circumcision party criticized him, saying, "You went to uncircumcised men and ate with them."** (Acts 11/2-3) Then he told them about his dream, of eating with the gentiles, **"But Peter began and explained it to them in order: "I was in the city of Joppa praying, and in a trance I saw a vision, something like a great sheet descending, being let down from heaven by its four corners, and it came down to me. Looking at it closely, I observed animals and beasts of prey and reptiles and birds of the air. And I heard a voice saying to me, 'Rise, Peter; kill and eat. But I said, 'By no means, Lord; for nothing common or unclean has ever entered my mouth. But the voice answered a second time from heaven, 'What God has made clean, do not call common. This happened three times, and all was drawn up again into heaven."** (Acts 11/4-10), and how the Holy Spirit came and asked him to go: **"And the Spirit told me to go with them, making no distinction. These six brothers also accompanied me."** (Acts 11/12)

After this convincing explanation from Peter, the disciples agreed to let him go to preach to the gentiles. **"When they heard these things they fell silent. And they glorified God, saying, "Then to the Gentiles also God has granted repentance that leads to life."** (Acts 11/18)

Thus, all these people, including Peter, knew nothing about Matthew's passage, which calls of baptizing the nations in the name of the Father, the Son and the Holy Spirit, why? Because Jesus (PBUH) did not mention it and they did not hear it from him, and if Jesus (PBUH) had said it, there would be no blame attached.

In addition, the disciples agreed with Paul that he would preach to the gentiles, and they would preach to the Jews. Paul said, **"when they saw that I had been entrusted with the gospel to the uncircumcised, just as Peter had been entrusted with the gospel to the circumcised. They gave the right hand of fellowship to Barnabas and me that we should go to the Gentiles and they to the circumcised."** (Galatia 2/7-9). How could they disobey Jesus' (PBUH) command - if Matthew's passage was true - and neglect preaching to the nations, and leave it only to Paul and Barnabas?

All of this evidence disproves Matthew's passage, and proves that it is a fabrication. Jesus (PBUH) did not speak these words.

Even if we overlook all that I have mentioned, there is nothing in the passage that says the Holy Trinity is one self. It talks about three different selves and using (and) indicates that he is talking about three different things. The correct meaning of Matthew's passage is "go by the name of Allah (S.W) and Jesus, his messenger, and the inspiration that Allah (S.W) sent to him, with Allah's (S.W) commandments."

Matthew's verse is similar to what Paul said in his Epistle to Timothy. However, Christians do not refer to it as evidence of the Trinity. Paul said, **"In the presence of God and of Christ Jesus and of the elect angels I charge you to keep these rules without prejudging, doing nothing from partiality"** (Tim. (1) 5/21). No one understands from this passage the divinity of the angels, or that they are the third hypostasis in the Trinity. The judgment on Paul's passage is the same as for Matthew's passage.

The Book of Exodus mentions the same when talking about calling the Children of Israel to believe in Allah (S.W) and Moses (PBUH), and no one believes that Allah (S.W) and Moses (PBUH) are one and equal. **"So the people feared the LORD, and they believed in the LORD and in his servant Moses."** (Exodus 14/31)

This way of expression is common in languages and books, as it is also in the Quran in many verses. **"O ye who believe! Believe in God and His Apostle, and the scripture which He hath sent to His Apostle and the scripture which He sent to those before (him)."** (Holy Quran 4:136)

A CRITICAL EXAMINATION OF THE TRINITY

If we cannot find any evidence supporting the Trinity, is there any evidence in the Holy Bible supporting the contrary, which is Monotheism?

One who studies the Holy Bible will find that the Trinity is a strange concept, and that the Holy Bible is full of obvious facts declaring monotheism in Christianity. There are many passages in the Holy Bible, which clearly declare that Monotheism was the belief of Jesus (PBUH), his disciples, and all the prophets (PBUT) before him.

First: Monotheistic Passages in the Old Testament

Monotheism is obvious in the Old Testament. Prophets (PBUT) spoke of it and remind us many times about it, and the passages strongly reassure this belief. Some of these passages are the following:

- What we find in the Book of Deuteronomy about Moses' (PBUH) commandments, which Allah (S.W) wrote on two stones and ordered the Children of Israel to keep, and Jesus (PBUH) after him confirmed them. **"Hear, O Israel: The LORD our God, the LORD is one. You shall love the LORD your God with all your heart and with all your soul and with all your might. And these words that I command you today shall be on your heart. You shall teach them diligently to your children, and shall talk of them when you sit in your house, and when you walk by the way, and when you lie down, and when you rise. You shall bind them as a sign on your hand, and they shall be as frontlets between your eyes. You shall write them on the doorposts of your house and on your gates."** (Deut. 6:4-9)

- **"I am the LORD your God, who brought you out of the land of Egypt, out of the house of slavery. You shall have no other gods before me."** (Deut. 5:6-7)

- Allah's (S.W) commandment to Moses (PBUH) and to the Children of Israel, **"I am the LORD your God, who brought you out of the land of Egypt, out of the house of slavery. You shall have no other gods before me. You shall not make for yourself a carved image, or any** likeness of anything that is in heaven above, or that is in the earth beneath, or that is in the water under the earth." (Ex. 20:2-4)

- In the First Book of Kings "that all the peoples of the earth may know that the LORD is God; there is no other." (Kings(1) 8:60)

- In Psalms "All the nations you have made shall come and worship before you, O Lord, and shall glorify your name For you are great and do wondrous things; you alone are God." (Psalms 86:9-10). That means He is the One and Only God, and no one – including Jesus (PBUH) - shares that with Him.

- In the Book of Isaiah, we read, "Before me no god was formed, nor shall there be any after me. I, I am the LORD, and besides me there is no savior. I declared and saved." (Isaiah 43:10 -12)

- "So now, O LORD our God, save us from his hand, that all the kingdoms of the earth may know that you alone are the LORD." (Isaiah 37:20)

- "I am the LORD, who made all things, who alone stretched out the heavens, who spread out the earth by myself." (Isaiah 44:24) this is totally contrary to the concept of the Trinity.

- "I am the LORD, and there is no other, besides me there is no God" (Isaiah 45:5)

- In Isaiah's prophecy, we read, "Thus says the LORD, the King of Israel and his Redeemer, the LORD of hosts: "I am the first and I am the last; besides me there is no god. Who is like me? Let him proclaim it. Let him declare and set it before me.... Is there a God besides me? There is no Rock; I know not any." (Isaiah 44:6 - 8)

- There are many other passages in the Old Testament. (Malachi 2:10, Kings 1 8:27, ...)

Second: Monotheistic Passages in the New Testament

The books of the New Testament clearly declare that Allah (S.W) is the One and Only God, Lord and Creator. The Gospels' writers indicate that Jesus (PBUH) and his disciples were the people who uttered these words.

- Jesus' saying, **"And call no man your father on earth, for you have one Father, who is in heaven. Neither be called instructors, for you have one instructor, the Christ."** (Matt 22: 9 – 10)

- **"A man came up to him, saying, "Teacher, what good deed must I do to have eternal life? And he said to him, "Why do you ask me about what is good? There is only one who is good."** (Matt 19:16-17)

- In the Book of John, **"When Jesus had spoken these words, he lifted up his eyes to heaven, and said, "Father, the hour has come; glorify your Son that the Son may glorify you. Since you have given him authority over all flesh, to give eternal life to all whom you have given him. And this is eternal life, that they know you the only true God, and Jesus Christ whom you have sent.** (John 17:1 – 3) . Therefore, there is no true God except One, and he is Allah (S.W).

- When trying to tempt Jesus (PBUH), the devil said, **"All these I will give you, if you will fall down and worship me." Then Jesus said to him, "Be gone, Satan! For it is written, "'You shall worship the Lord your God and him only shall you serve."** (Matt. 4:10) the same is in Luke. (Luke 4:8)

- Jesus (PBUH) told the Jews, **"You are doing what your father did." They said to him, "We were not born of sexual immorality. We have one Father--even God." Jesus said to them, "If God were your Father, you would love me, for I came from God and I am here. I came not of my own accord, but he sent me."** (John 8:41- 42)

These passages and many others speak about One God, and there is nothing in them that speak about three beings uniting in one person as the Christians claim.

The Trinity is a Mystery Unacceptable by the Mind

With this clear contradiction between the Church Councils' decisions and the Bible's monotheistic passages, Christians had to use their minds to solve this matter. They had to solve these contradictions, which are impossible to put together, and explain to people the issue about the three who are one, and about the one who is three.

In addition, with the weakness of this dogma, and the impossibility of understanding it by the human mind, Christians have no choice but to say that the Trinity is a mystery that is impossible to comprehend. Moreover, some Christians confess that Christianity conflicts with the mind.

Saint Augustine said, "I believe because that is unacceptable by our mind".

Kier Cougard said, "Each attempt to make Christianity a credible religion would result in destroying it." In 'The Christian Teachings' we read, "It is not allowed to ask about God's secrets, because we cannot comprehend the belief's secrets."

In his book, 'The Catholic Teachings', priest De Grout said, "The Holy Trinity is a puzzle in the truest sense, and our mind cannot digest a Tri-God, but this what the inspiration taught us."

Describing the Trinity, Zaki Shnouda said, "It is one of the divine mysteries, which is impossible for our mind to comprehend."

Father James Ted said, "Christianity is beyond the mind's understanding"

Priest Anis Shoroush said, "One in three and three in one, are mysteries you do not have to understand, but you have to accept."

In his book 'Eternity Secret", priest Tawfiq Jayed made understanding the Trinity impossible, and there is no point in trying to do so, because, as he said, "whoever tries to understand it completely, is like he who wants to put the ocean's water in his palm."[1]

---

[1]- Christ (PBUH) Between Facts and Imagination, Mohammad Wasfi, pp 139, The Debate of Time, Ahmad Deedat, pp 105, Christian Creeds Between the Quran and Reason, Hashem Jodah, pp 153. A Study on the Torah and the Gospel, Kamel Saafan, pp 235 Christianity Without Christ, Kamel Saafan, pp 127

Due to all of this misleading, the truth will disappear, which is that the Trinity is an impossible creed to understand; not because of the weakness of our mind, but because it conflicts with common sense and human nature.

THE STORY OF MONOTHEISM AND THE TRINITY IN THE HISTORY OF CHRISTIANITY

"And behold! Allah will say: "O Jesus the son of Mary! Didst thou say unto men, worship me and my mother as gods in derogation of Allah.?" He will say: "Glory to Thee! never could I say what I had no right (to say). Had I said such a thing, thou wouldst indeed have known it. Thou knowest what is in my heart, though I know not what is in Thine. For Thou knowest in full all that is hidden. "Never said I to them aught except what Thou didst command me to say, to wit, 'worship Allah, my Lord and your Lord'; and I was a witness over them whilst I dwelt amongst them; when Thou didst take me up Thou wast the Watcher over them, and Thou art a witness to all things." (Holy Quran 5: 116- 117)

If Jesus (PBUH) and his contemporaries did not claim that he is divine, how did these creeds come into Christianity?

Answering the question, I say, "It was Paul who inserted them into Christianity." It was Paul, the Jew, who was the enemy of Christianity, who claimed seeing Jesus (PBUH) after Allah (S.W) lifted him up to heaven. He took these creeds from many pagans, which make some people holy, considering them sons of God. **"And the Christians call Christ the son of God. That is a saying from their mouth; (in this) they but imitate what the unbelievers of old used to say. God's curse be on them: how they are deluded away from the Truth!"** (Holy Quran 9: 30).

The Importance of Paul in Christianity

Paul is the most famous writer amongst the New Testament writers, and he is absolutely the most important evangelist. He wrote fourteen Epistles, which are almost half of the New Testament, and only in these Epistles do we find many of the Christian creeds. Paul is the founder of Christianity and its creeds, and he is the only evangelist who claimed prophethood among the others.

Paul's Epistles are the supportive pillar of this altered Christianity. His Epistles were the first written documents in the New Testament, and are slightly similar to the others, especially the Book of John.

The Church had rejected many other epistles that conflict with Paul's Christianity, which suppressed Jesus' and his disciples' Christianity.

The influence of Paul in Christianity is undeniable. That made Michael Hart, in his celebrated work, *"the 100, a ranking of the Most Influential Persons in History"*; place Paul among the most important influential people in history. He placed Jesus (PBUH) third, and Paul sixth.

Regarding the reason for placing Prophet Mohammad (PBUH) at the followers are the majority on earth, Michael Hart said, "Christianity was not established by one person but by two: Jesus and Paul. Therefore, the honor of establishing it must be divided between both of them. Jesus had established the moral principles of Christianity, its spiritual views, and everything about human behavior; and Paul was the one who developed its Theology."

He added, "Jesus did not preach any of Paul's sayings, and Paul is considered responsible for Jesus' Divinity". Hart also brought to our attention that Paul did not use the term 'Son of Man', which Jesus (PBUH) used to call himself.

In his book 'The Expanded Universe', Sir Arthur Findlay said, "Paul was the one who established the religion called Christianity."

Paul and Jesus' Divinity

If the Gospels – excluding the Book of John – have nothing to prove Jesus' (PBUH) divinity, Paul's Epistles are full of passages that exaggerate Jesus (PBUH) and passages considering him as a rare and unique person. Then, what did Paul say about Jesus (PBUH), did he consider him as a prophet, God incarnate or…?

Reading Paul's Epistles carefully, we find contradictory answers from one Epistle to another, for some passages declare his humanity (PBUH), and others declare his divinity. Does this contradiction come from Paul's fickle changes according to his listeners, was it because of his thought development about Jesus (PBUH), or was it because of these Epistles' alterations and fabrications? All these are just possibilities, without certainty.

Among these passages, which talk about Jesus (PBUH) as a servant of Allah (S.W) but different from other people because he was loved and chosen by Allah (S.W), Paul said, **"For there is one God, and** there is one mediator between God and men, the man Christ Jesus." (Ti.1 2:5)

Confessing the Oneness of Allah (S.W), Paul said, "to keep the commandment unstained and free from reproach until the appearing of our Lord Jesus Christ. which he will display at the proper time--he who is the blessed and only Sovereign, the King of kings and Lord of lords. who alone has immortality." (Ti.1 6:14 - 16). Thus, Jesus is lord, but only Allah (S.W) is the Lord of lords. These passages and many more talk about Jesus (PBUH) as being human, yet different from others; for, Allah (S.W) loves him and chose him to deliver His message.

Other passages are full of Jesus' (PBUH) exaggeration, making him – almost - a real son of Allah (S.W), which may indicate that there is a difference between Jesus' son-ship and other son-ships in the Holy Bible. This is clear in some other passages, which consider Jesus (PBUH) as God's image or God incarnate.

He said, "By sending his own Son in the likeness of sinful flesh" (Rom. 8:3)

"He who did not spare his own Son but gave him up" (Rom. 8:32)

He added, "God sent forth his Son, born of woman" (Gal. 4:4) which indicates a real son-ship of Jesus (PBUH), for, all believers are sons of God – metaphorically – and are born of women.

"He is the image of the invisible God, the firstborn of all creation." (Col. 1:15)

"Who, though he was in the form of God, did not count equality with God a thing to be grasped. But made himself nothing, taking the form of a servant, being born in the likeness of men." (Phil. 2:6-7)

"Great indeed, we confess, is the mystery of godliness: He was manifested in the flesh" (Tim.1 3:16)

"And at the proper time manifested in his word through the preaching with which I have been entrusted by the command of God our Savior." (Titus 1:3). Therefore, Paul is the only one among the New Testament writers who talked of Jesus' (PBUH) divinity.

Scholars talked about the conditions that made Paul say what he said about Jesus' (PBUH) divinity, and the resources, from which Paul derived this belief.

The areas, in which Paul preached, were full of myths that spread and were accepted by the naïve, who were the majority of the people at that time. In addition, those communities were idolatrous; they believed in multiple gods, their incarnation, and their death. In their journey to Lystra, Paul and Barnabas performed some miracles: **"And when the crowds saw what Paul had done, they lifted up their voices, saying in Lycaonian, "The gods have come down to us in the likeness of men! Barnabas they called Zeus, and Paul, Hermes."** (Acts 14/11-12) Zeus and Hermes, according to the editors of the Holy Bible Dictionary, are names for two of the Greek gods; the first is the great god and the second is the god of eloquence.

Thus, those simple people believed that Paul and Barnabas were gods, just because they did some miracles. Moreover, the Book of Acts mentions that the priests offered a sacrifice for them, but they did not because Paul and Barnabas rejected that. (Acts 14:13-18)

What would those people say about Jesus (PBUH) who brought the dead to life, he himself rose from the dead, and performed many miracles?

The idea of the incarnated gods was acceptable for pagans, who made dates and celebrations for the incarnated gods' birth, death, and resurrection. Therefore, Paul spread the story of God's descent to the earth for the Romans to see, and to be close to them.

The churches in which Paul preached adopted and accepted this belief more than other churches, accepting the idea of the human God, as it was worshipping idols before that.

Jesus' (PBUH) divinity became an official belief in Christianity after the First Nicene Council, which decided Jesus' divinity, and the First Council of Constantinople completed the Trinity when they deified the Holy Spirit.

First: The First Nicene Council

In 325 C.E., by the order of the Pagan emperor Constantine, who declared a few years before, the law of the religious indulgence in the empire -The Nicene Council - was formed.

Constantine realized that the conflict between Christian churches was affecting the people in the empire, and threatening the existence of the country. Thus, he decided to set up a general council gathering all Christian parties. He personally set up the council, and 2048 priests from different churches were present. The negotiations lasted for three months without agreeing on one opinion.

The emperor conciliated the conflicting parties, and they presented the Nicene Creed, which made the belief in Jesus' (PBUH) divinity an official belief for Christians and then for the Roman Empire.

The Nicene Council did not discuss the Holy Spirit or his divinity. The negotiations about him continued between churches until they settled the matter at the First Council of Constantinople.

Second: The First Council of Constantinople

The First Council of Constantinople was formed in 381 C.E., to discuss Macedonius, the Arian who was the bishop of Constantinople, who denied the divinity of the Holy Spirit. He said, "The Holy Spirit is a divine work spread in the world, he is not a divine person, who is different from the Father and the Son."

The council was formed by order of the emperor Theodosius I (D.395 C.E.). One hundred and fifty bishops were present, deciding to annul the Arian belief. In addition, they decided that the Holy Spirit is Allah's (S.W) spirit and His life, and that he is the third hypostasis of the Trinity, and they added one passage to the Nicene Creed; thus, the Trinity became the official creed of Christianity.

There were many monotheists, who in spite of their minor contribution and presence refuted the Trinity and Jesus' (PBUH) divinity even after the Nicene Council for many centuries, despite the existence of the church's power and authority.

The reason for this minor contribution and presence was the existence of the Inquisitions and the churches' power. It is enough here to mention some of these parties, whom the church considered heretics for denying Jesus' (PBUH) divinity and the Trinity. They were the Nazarenes, the Arians, the Ebonites, the Apollinaris, and the Nestorians.[1]

Monotheism After the Reformation

With the reduction of the authority and the power of the church, the unitary parties reappeared, and the Trinity became unstable. This was Martin Luther and others' expression. Luther said, "The Trinity is a weak expression, lacks convincing power, and is never mentioned in the holy books."

In his book "The History of the Unitarians", Filbert said, "Calvin announced that, "it is more suitable for the Nicene Creed, which was issued by the Nicene Council, to be a song instead of being a statement of belief."

When Calvin wrote his book, "The Institutes of Christian Religion", he seldom mentioned the Trinity.

At the beginning of the twentieth century, the number of Unitarians increased; their contribution became more and yielded about four hundred churches in Britain and its colonies; the same happened in the United States. Besides two theological colleges in Britain that teach Unitarianism - Manchester and Oxford - another two colleges exist in America - one in Chicago and the other in Prickly in California. There are around one hundred and sixty churches or colleges in Hungary, and many others in the Christian European countries. [1]

In 1921 C.E, at a conference held in Oxford, which was attended by many religious scholars, the chairperson was the bishop of Carlyle, Dr. Rachel. He said in his speech, "That his reading of the Holy Bible, does not make him believe in Jesus as God, and for what is mentioned in John's Gospel, which is never mentioned in the synoptic, cannot be considered as historical." He also believed that all that was said about Jesus (PBUH): his birth of a virgin, healing diseases, or saying that his spirit preceded human existence - do not

---

[1]- The Church History, Eusebius, pp 130, 343
[1]- Monotheistic Christians in History, Ahmad Abdul Wahab, pp 45-53

mean his divinity. Many of the attendees also shared with him the same opinion.

Emil Lord says, "Jesus did not believe himself to be more than a prophet, even though sometimes he believed that he was less than a prophet. He never mentioned what makes one believe - that he has different views and thoughts from those that are human. Jesus used a new word to express his modesty when he said that he is the Son of Man. In the past, prophets called themselves sons of man to show the difference between them and God."

In 1977 C.E., seven theologians wrote a famous book titled, "The Myth of the Incarnated God". In this book, we find that "This group approved that the books of the Holy Bible were written by a group of people in different circumstances, and their words could not be considered as divine. Those who contributed in writing this book believe that there will be some development in theology by the end of the twentieth century."

Eight theologians in Britain wrote a book called "Jesus is Not the Son of God". They confirmed what the first book mentioned - they said "The possibility of a human becoming God is unlikely and unbelievable nowadays." [1]

In April 1984 C.E, London's Weekend Television had an interview with Bishop David Jenkins, who holds the fourth position among thirty-nine bishops, which are the top of the Anglican Church. He mentioned that, "Jesus' divinity is not a definite fact, and that he does not believe that the virgin birth and Jesus' resurrection are historical events." (Meaning they are untrue).

His words had a huge effect on those who follow the Protestant Church. The Daily-News newspaper gave a questionnaire to thirty-one bishops, out of the thirty-nine, about what Jenkins has said. They published the result of that questionnaire on 25/6/1984 C.E, and it was as follows:

"11 bishops insisted that Christians must consider Jesus both God and human. While 19 said that, "it is enough to consider Jesus as God's high representative". Nine bishops doubted the idea of Jesus' resurrection, and said that it was a series of experiences or feelings,

---

[1]- Differences in the Holy Bible Translations, Ahmad Abdul Wahab, pp 113

which convinced his followers that he was alive among them. Fifteen bishops said, "The miracles, which are mentioned in the New Testament, were added to Jesus' story later". This means it cannot be evidence of his divinity.[1]

Thus, the church, and its bishops, doubt the idea of Jesus' (PBUH) divinity and reject it. They confess that it is an additional belief to Christianity. They also affirm that neither Jesus (PBUH) nor his disciples knew it, and that Paul, those who followed him and wrote the Gospels and the Epistles, and the church councils, originated it.

From the above, we find that Monotheism is an original movement in the Christian community. This movement renews whenever those who are faithful look in their Holy Books. It refreshes their vision, and announces the clear truth, that there is no God but Allah (S.W).

---

[1]- The Church of England Bishops and Jesus' Divinity, Ahmad Deedat, pp 29-31, Differences in the Holy Bible Translations, Ahmad Abdul Wahab, pp 114-115

THE ORIGIN OF THE CONCEPT OF JESUS' DIVINITY

Christian beliefs were completed in the forth century, after deifying Jesus (PBUH) and the Holy Spirit, and confirming the Holy Bible. Paul established a new Christianity after Jesus (PBUH), so where did Paul and the later Church Councils, derive these new beliefs?

To answer that question we quote what Charles Gene Pier said in his book "Christianity, its Beginning and its Development", he said, "Detailed study of Paul's longer Epistles, results in finding a mixture of strange ideas, both Jewish and idolatrous Greek concepts.

To explain and illustrate further, we review some of the old religions before Christianity, to show the similarity between ancient Paganism and Christian Paganism. This similarity has touched the basis and the branches of Christian creeds, so we could know the origin and the source, from which Christianity takes its beliefs and creeds.

First: God's Incarnation in Ancient Pagan Religions

Believing in an incarnated God, the second divine hypostasis of God, incarnated to forgive people's sins, is an old and known belief in ancient religions, such as Hinduism. In his book "India", the historian Allen said, "Krishna is the greatest of all the incarnated gods, and much superior to them, for they were only partly divine, but He (Krishna) appeared as god in a human figure.

Mentioned in the Indian book "Baha Kavat Boron", Krishna said, "I will incarnate in Yedwa house, and come out from Devaki womb, I will be born and die, the time has come to show my power, and relieve the earth of its burden". Therefore, the Hindus considered him a divine incarnation that made him worthy of worship.

The prominent historian Dwain talked about Buddha in his book "The Myths of the Torah, the Gospel, and Their Similarity in Other Religions". He said, "Buddha was born of the virgin Maya, whom the Buddhists in India and other countries worship. They say about him, "He left the heaven and descended to appear as a human figure, as mercy to people to save them from their sins and to guide them".

The historian Dawn also mentioned that the Europeans were astonished when they went to Comorine, west of India, from seeing the people worship a god called Silvahana, and he was born of a virgin.

Among humans that people said were incarnate, is the god Fuhi in China, and Wisten Nonick and Hwankty, and others. People used to say of the god Bromesus, "He was a real man and a real god.[1]

Thus, we can say that God's incarnation existed in ancient Pagan religions before Christianity, from which Paul and the Councils took the belief of Jesus' divinity.

Second: The Incarnation for Forgiveness and Salvation

What Christians believe about the reason for the incarnation corresponds with that of the ancient Pagan religions, as Christians say, the incarnation was for Jesus to die and save humanity from their sins.

The prominent scholar Hawk quoted the same about the Indian incarnated gods. He said, "Indians believe that, one of the gods had incarnated, and sacrificed himself to save the people from their sins".

The same was quoted about Buddha, whom the historian Morris William mentioned in his book (Indian Religion), "of his mercy (meaning Buddha) he left the heaven and came to the earth, to save humanity from their sins and pains, and from the punishment they deserve."

Dawn mentions in his book "The Myths of the Torah, the Gospel, and Their Similarity in Other Religions"; Indians call Bokhas, the son of Jupiter, the nations' savior."

The same was said about Hercules, Mithra, the Persians' savior, and Bacob, the Mexican crucified god, and others, whom their followers believed to be gods, incarnated to forgive sins.[1]

---

[1]- Paganism in Christianity, Mohammad Taher Attenneer, pp 47-56
[1]- Paganism in Christianity, Mohammad Taher Attenneer, pp 29-38, Christianity, Ahmad Shalaby, pp 151, 158

Third: The Incarnated God and Creation

Similar to the Christians' belief that Jesus the Son is the creator, is the ancient religions' belief in their incarnated gods. The Indians' sacred books mention that "Krishna the son of god from the virgin Divacki, is the second divine hypostasis in the Holy Trinity, created heavens and earth, and for them (the believers) he is the first and the last".

In the holy book "Bhagwad Geeta", Krishna said to his student Argon, "I am the god of the all creations, I created them and humans... know me, I am the creator of humans".

The Chinese believe that the Father created nothing, and the son Latotho, who was born from a virgin, created everything.

In their prayers to Adermizd, the Persians say, "to Adermizd I pray, for he created everything that was created or will be. He is the wise, the strong, who created the sky, the sun, the moon and the stars."

The Assyrians believe the same of the first son "Nerdock", also those who deify "Adonis", and "Laokion", and others.

Likewise, in the old Egyptian tradition, the god "Atom" created every living thing by the word, which created life and everything edible, and all what humans love or hate.[1]

Forth: Eternity and Immortality of the Incarnated Gods

John described Jesus in his Revelation, as the first and the last, and the Alpha and Omega. This description corresponds exactly with the description of the idolatrous and their incarnated gods, of which they believe in their eternity and immortality.

In the Indian book "Geeta", Krishna said, "It never happened that I was nonexistent, I made everything, and I am the everlasting and the eternal, the creator who existed before everything. I am the strong ruler, who has power over the universe; I am the first, the middle, and the last of everything'.

---

[1]- Paganism in Christianity, Mohammad Taher Attenneer, pp 119-120

From Argon's prayers to Krishna, "you are the everlasting, the great, whom we must know, who controls the beings; you are the god who existed before gods".

The book "Fishno Borani" describes him: "he has no start, no middle, and no end".

Mentioned in the Indian scriptures about Buddha: "he is Alpha and Omega, there is no start or end to his existence, and he is the god, the owner, the powerful and the everlasting". The same was said about Lawken, Lawtz, Armizd, Zios, and many others, who were called the "Alpha and Omega". [1]

Fifth: The Dates of Gods' Birth, Worship, and Traditions

Not only do Christian beliefs correspond with other religions on some issues, but also on worshipping and dates as well. The idolatrous believe, in spite of the differences of their gods, that their incarnated gods were born on 25th of December, such as the god Mithra and others.

That is what the Orthodox Christians say of their dates. It was fixed in 530 C.E. by the priest Deunesus. He wanted to draw Christians away from the idolatrous celebrations, and occupy them with Christian celebration. The same happened in many other idolatrous celebrations, so the Christians took the dates and the traditions from them.

In his book, "The History of the Anglican Church", Priest Beid quoted Pope Gregory's first speech, (601C.E), in which he quoted Pope Mellitus's advice, which forbade the destruction of the idolatrous temples. In addition, he believed in turning them away from worshipping the devil to worship the true God, to clean the people's hearts of sins, and make it easier for them to visit the temples, which they used to visit. [1]

Thus, the new Christian will not find any difference, in the place or the content, between Christianity and what he/she believes, which will make it easier to spread Christianity.

---

[1]- Paganism in Christianity, Mohammad Taher Attenneer, pp 120-121

[1] - Frank Discussion Between the Servant of Allah and the Servant of Christ, Abdul Wadoud Shalaby, pp 67-72, Christianity, Ahmad Shalaby, pp 83, The True Christianity That Christ Taught, Alaa Abu Bakr, pp 191-192

The Trinity in Ancient Paganism

Not only did Christians take the belief of Jesus' divinity and God's incarnation from the idolatrous, but they also took their belief in the Trinity.

To prove that, we will review the ancient pagan nations' history that was before the time of Jesus (PBUH). History proves that many of the idolatrous believed in the Trinity before Christians, and what the Christians say about the Trinity was taken from these nations with little alteration in the Trinity hypostasis, by changing the names of the idolatrous Trinity.

The belief of the triple god existed four thousand years before the birth of Christ (PBUH). The Babylonians believed in it, when they divided the gods into three groups, (the god of sky, the god of earth, and the god of sea).

Then, the Trinity developed as it is now in Christianity, in the tenth century before Christ. The Indians believe that their Trinity consists of Brahma, Fishna, and Seva, and these three are one.

Mentioned in the pious Atnis prayers, "oh, three gods know that I believe in one god. Tell me, which of you is the real god, to pray for and present my vow? Then the three gods appeared and said to him: you, the worshipper, know that there is no difference between us, the three you see is in the shape and the sameness, but there is only one divine person in the three".

Found in Indian remains, was an idol with three heads and one body, indicating the Trinity.

The Trinity was known by the ancient pagans, such as the Egyptian Trinity (Ozirous, Izes, and Hoars), the Persian Trinity (Ormizd, Mitras, and Ahraman), the Scandinavian Trinity (Aowen, Tora, and Freie), and the Mexican Trinity (Tzikliboka, Ahotzlipo Shtiki, and Tlakoma). The Greek philosophers, whose belief was similar to the Christians', also believed in their Trinity (existence, knowledge, life), and many others, which will take too long to mention.[1]

---

[1]- Paganism in Christianity, Mohammad Taher Attenneer, pp 13-23, Christianity, Ahmad Shalaby, pp 118-120, A Study on the Torah and The Gospel, Kamel Saafan, pp 81, 228

Even the Nicene Creed, which the Nicene Council produced, was from old religions. The historian Malver quoted from the Indian books about their belief, saying, "we believe in Bsafstri (the sun), the controller of all, who created heavens and the earth, and in his only son "Ani" (the fire), light from light, begotten not made, being of one substance with the Father, was incarnated by Faya (the spirit) of the virgin Maya. We believe in Fayo, the spirit who proceeded from the Father and the son, who is the father, and the son glorifies and kneels to him."

The Encyclopedia Britannica mentions that, "the concept of the Trinity is of Greek origin, with Jewish input and is a strange mixture made by Christians, because the religious concepts are taken from the Holy Bible, but they are filled with foreign philosophies.

The concepts (The father, the son, and the Holy Spirit) come from the Jews, and the last concept (The Holy Spirit) was rarely used by Jesus.

Leon Joteh says, "Christianity absorbed many ideas and concepts from Greek philosophy. Christian theology is taken from the same source, which is Platonism, and that is why we find many similarities between them".

Greek philosophy spread through Alexandria, where Plato the Alexandrian was (207C.E). He believed in the treble (God, mind, spirit). Thus, the Alexandrian saints were the first to believe in the Trinity and defend it.

Will Durant and others said, that paganism spread through Rome. Will Durant also said, "When Christianity conquered Rome, the new religion was influenced by the old pagan rituals, such as the titles, the great cardinal, and the worshipping of the great mother."

In his book "Christian Paganism", Robertson supports this idea; he believes that those beliefs arrived in Rome, brought by the Persians, in the year 70 B.C.E.
Others believe that those beliefs spread by the ancient Pharaohs ideology passed to Christianity because of their close proximity.

Other scholars believe that the spread of these concepts was from Torsos, which had great schools of Greek literature, and was where Paul grew up and was influenced by these concepts.[1]

The spread of paganism into Christianity is a clear fact, which made some honest and brave writers confess.

Among them, the archeologist Garslafe Creny, in his book "Ancient Egyptian Religion", he said, "The Trinity was added to the real Christianity, and it was taken from the pagan Pharaohs' belief".

In his book, "Christian Paganism" the prominent scholar Robertson talked in detail about Christian adoption of paganism. He said, "It is a pleasure to say, that among those who criticized my book, no one disagreed with the facts that I mentioned in it, and this convinced me that most Christian beliefs are taken from paganism."

The authors of the book, "The Myth of God's Incarnation", mentioned the same; "The belief that Jesus is God, the son of God, or God incarnated in him, is no more than pagan myth and legend."[2]

From that, I can say that the Trinity is a pagan adoption, which led away from natural instinct, strayed from the prophets' guidance, and worshipped other than Allah (S.W), the greatest.

Allah the Greatest tells us, about the origin of Christian disbelief, He says, **"The Jews call 'Uzair a son of God, and the Christians call Christ the son of God. That is a saying from their mouth; (in this) they but imitate what the unbelievers of old used to say. God's curse be on them: how they are deluded away from the Truth!"** (Holy Quran 9:30).

---

[1]- Paganism in Christianity, Mohammad Taher Attenneer, pp 173, Christianity, Ahmad Shalaby, pp 150, Judaism and Christianity, Mohammad Diaurahman Al Aathamy, 282, 299, 414-415

[2]- Frank Discussion Between the Servant of Allah and the Servant of Christ, Abdul Wadoud Shalaby, pp 67-73, Christianity, Ahmad Shalaby, pp 152, The True Christianity That Christ Taught, Alaa Abu Bakr, pp 139, Christ in the Quran, the Torah and the Gospel, Abdul Kareem El Khateeb, pp 137, Monotheistic Christian Creeds Between Islam and Christianity, Husni Al Ateer, pp 19-20

Conclusion

Thus, I have reached the end of this book, hopefully answering my question, is Allah (S.W) one or three?

We saw, while studying the passages of the Holy Bible that Jesus (PBUH) was one of the greatest messengers of Allah (S.W). He (PBUH) did not claim Lordship or divinity, and he did not stop, even for a moment, worshipping Allah (S.W), and commanding his people to do the same.

It is certain that Christians' claimed evidence of Jesus' (PBUH) divinity is a mirage, easily disproved by a little examination of the Holy Bible passages, which prove Jesus' (PBUH) humanity and prophethood.

We also know, following this critical study, the source, from which Paul derived this pagan belief, by which he wanted to alter Christianity by making it a pagan religion. He left the path of Jesus (PBUH) and his disciples, and made Christianity appear in a new style. Thus, the disciples and the apostles disappeared during the Roman persecution, to await the new dawn that is the last Testament, which is Islam and its great Prophet Mohammad (PBUH).

While thanking the reader for reading these lines, I invite him to read the next episode of this series "True Guidance and Light", with the title, "Did Jesus (PBUH) Sacrifice His Life on the Cross?"

O Allah, show and guide us to the truth, that we argue about, indeed, you guide whom you will, to the straight path. Amen.

Sources and References:

- The Holy Quran

- The Holy Bible, English Standard Version.1981

- The Holy Bible, The Middle East Holy Bible's publishers edition, Protestant's copy

- The Holy Bible, The Middle East Holy Bible's publishers edition, Orthodox' copy

- The Holy Bible, the Jesuit Priesthood edition, Catholic's copy, issued by the Jesuit fathers, and distributed by the Holy Bible's organizations in the East, Beirut. *(Translated from the Good News Bible, Today's English Version, 2nd Edition 1992)*

- The Bible in Basic English, 1965

- Douay-Rheims Bible, 1899

- Darby Bible, 1889

- The Holy Bible (The Hebrew Holy Scriptures and the Greek Holy Scriptures) new world translation, (Jehovah witnesses' edition)

- The Samaritan Torah, Translated by Priest Abu Al Hassan Isaac Assory, Published by Ahmad Hijazy Al Saqa (1st edition) Al Ansar publishing, Cairo, 1398 lunar calendar

- The Gospel of Barnabas, Translation of Khalil Saada. Al Wathaeq publishing's edition. Kuwait, 1406 lunar calendar,

---

- John the Baptist Between Islam and Christianity, Ahmad Hijazy Al Saqa, 1st edition, Al Turath Al Araby publishing, 1399 lunar calendar

- The Truth Revealed, Rahamtu Allah Al Hindi, revised by Muhammad Ahmad Malkawy, Al Hadith publishing, Cairo, 1404 lunar calendar

- The Clerical Knowledge Encyclopedia, 3rd edition, Al Thaqafa publishing 1995

- The History of the Christian Ideology, the Priest Dr Hana Gerges Al Khodary, Dar Al Thaqafa publishing, Cairo, 1981

- The Interpretation of John's Gospel, Priest Athnasius, 4th edition, Dar AlJeel, Cairo, 1995

- The Holy Bible's Dictionary, a selection of professors and theologians, editors, Botros Abdul Malik, John Alexander Thomson, Ibrahim Mattar, 9th edition, Al Thaqafa publishing, 1994

- The Practical Interpretation of the Holy Bible, group of theology scholars, Cairo

Index: